Management

Skills for IT

Professionals

Management

Skills for IT

Professionals

George M. Doss

PRENTICE HALL
Paramus, NJ

Library of Congress Cataloging-in-Publication Data

Doss, George M.
    Management skills for IT professionals / George M. Doss.
       p. cm.
    ISBN 0-13-032009-9
    1. Management information technology.   2. Industrial management—Data processing.
 I. Title.

    HD30.213 .D67 2001
    658—dc21   00-045638

Acquisitions Editor: *Susan McDermott*
Production Editor: *Jacqueline Roulette*
Formatting/Interior Design: *Robyn Beckerman*

This publication is designed to provide accurate and authoritative information in regard to the subject matter covered. It is sold with the understanding that the publisher is not engaged in rendering legal, accounting, or other professional service. If legal advice or other expert assistance is required, the services of a competent professional person should be sought.

—From a Declaration of Principles jointly adopted by a Committee of the American Bar Association and a Committee of Publishers and Associations

Printed in the United States of America

10 9 8 7 6 5 4 3 2 1

ISBN 0-13-032009-9

ATTENTION: CORPORATIONS AND SCHOOLS

Prentice Hall books are available at quantity discounts with bulk purchase for educational, business, or sales promotional use. For information, please write to: Prentice Hall Special Sales, 240 Frisch Court, Paramus, New Jersey 07652. Please supply: title of book, ISBN, quantity, how the book will be used, and date needed.

PRENTICE HALL
Paramus, NJ 07652

http://www.phdirect.com

Contents

Section 2
Managing Individuals   45

Section 3
IT Team Management   111

Section 4
Customers and Vendors and an IT Project   167

Section 5
Communication Skills   189

Section 6
Project Management Tools   225

Dedication

This book is dedicated to the coaches, players, and goalies of the National Hockey League. The NHL is one of the few places where you can see a visual instance of dynamic project management. You have measurable goals. You have skill and performance benchmarks. You have effective oral communication even if it is mostly in four-letter words, or their variants, in multiple languages. You can get a rapid comprehension of team dynamics as lines move on and off the ice. One might even have a strategic manager (general manager), tactical manager (coach), and operational managers (especially team captains, assistant team captains, and franchise players).

Measurable goals determine the level of success. There are goals both for the team and for individuals. Measurable team goals by level of success are as follows:

- Win the Stanley Cup (to the man this is the only goal)
- Win the Conference Title
- Have the most points in the League at the end of the season
- Have the most points in the team's conference at the end of the season
- Have the most points in the team's division at the end of the season
- Have sufficient points to be in the top eight teams of a conference at the end of the season

The 82 games (milestones) are just commentary on these goals. One can learn that a loss anytime can be a risk. One loss can leave a team in ninth place in the conference at the end of the season with no chance for the Cup.

What is important to me as a viewer of the process is not only that each milestone can be so exciting, but also to see how coaches manage illnesses, slumps, and penalties.

Introduction

This book is entitled *Management Skills for IT Professionals,* but what does the title mean to you as the reader? IT as used in the book means information technology that in today's electronic jargon is a network technology that includes a system (a structure that consists of people, software, and hardware) that uses computers to transfer data or text from one location to another. Management here means a systematic process to achieve a defined measurable goal or goals within a prescribed time and within budget with limited resources, that is equipment, material, and skills.

Notice that a *person* is not considered a *resource.* A person is head-count. A resource, or skill, is what a person can do at a given level in a given amount of time, with a certain degree of proficiency, which is important to a manager. A skill is a capability and a proficiency that results in an observable positive result or a negative consequence. Occasionally a person might confuse a trait with a skill. A trait is a characteristic such as having empathy. Traits play a major role in "touch-and-feel" management. This type of management can play a role in achieving desired results; however, the book does not cover this management type because in many cases the overall results of a trait cannot be observed. A professional is a person who is an acknowledged spokesperson for a given field that can be defined as being very broad or very narrow. In summary, this book is about capabilities (skills) to achieve observable or measurable results (goals) using a systematic process (management) in a computerized environment (IT) engaged in the specific activity of information technology and systems. Management is considered in this book in two situations—day-to-day operations and projects.

A *professional,* as used in this book, means a person qualified for a specific occupation or field; in this case, the field can be labeled either *information systems* (network and Internet) or *information technology* (software and hardware). A part of being qualified is not only knowing technical information, but also knowing how to manage the people in an IT organization or a project that has IT implications across functional areas. To manage means to use the correct skill set at the correct time. It can be to pull, push, control, direct, lead, supervise, or many other actions to achieve a goal.

Because the focus of this book is on skills, this idea needs to be clarified now, not later. A skill might be considered ability, dexterity, proficiency, an art, a trade, or a technique. To add further to the confusion, one could include in the list also the following: adeptness, competency, deftness, expertise, facility, and talent. Whatever word you want to use, the essential points are a skill can be duplicated somewhat and has observable or measurable results.

There are five basic steps in acquiring any skill. These five steps are as follows:

- Assessing yourself as to your competency

- Learning the skill from either reading or observing

- Analyzing the skill using examples

- Practicing the skill in an environment where you can get feedback

- Applying the skill in the work environment

In today's flexible and lean organization, the parameters between functions are blending. As a result, you may find yourself becoming far more involved in working on cross-functional projects or functioning as a leader of multidisciplinary teams, even though the term "project manager" figures nowhere in your title. To be effective in this situation you need to acquire new skills that extend beyond your functional role. This might be more important to an IT manager who acts as a project manager more often than any other type of functional manager. There is a general lack of technical comprehension among other managers about a computer network system and a greater need for direction.

Throughout the book, labels are going to be used for a project manager type with or without a given set of skills. The "with" usually represents the positive, while the "without" usually represents the negative. No person is a single management type all the time. Beware when one is considered in such a manner. In reality, during a project you should use many different management types. At a specific moment, you could be labeled as several types by the same person. The labels are used in this book for discussing a certain set of skills that give a perception of the manager.

This book offers you an opportunity to acquire the relevant practical people skills and techniques that perhaps can stimulate that which is the best in you.

PEOPLE SIDE OF PROJECT MANAGEMENT

Project management has two sides, managing the process and managing the people. This book emphasizes managing the people more than managing the process. While one is managing the administrative process, one is always managing people. A part of the administrative process is the managing of e-mail, but that requires written communication skills beyond the knowledge of how to send e-mails. Some areas of the project management process that have to be considered in using effective skills to achieve successful project management include the following:

- People and the process
    - Alliances
    - Authority
    - National, corporate, and individual culture and values
    - Organizational relationships
    - Project team organization
    - Responsibilities
    - Team dynamics
- Project leader or manager
    - Consistency
    - Influence and persuasion

— Leadership skills and principles

— Model for success

— Motivation techniques

— Problem solving styles

— Self-assessment (strengths and weakness identification)

— Situation leadership (management style adaptation)

• Project team organization

— Assessment

— Behavior dynamics

— Conflict management

— Creativity

— Decision-making and consensus

— Delegation of responsibility

— Empowerment

— Management interfaces

— Participation and involvement

— Performance

— Problem solving styles

— Selection and development

— Strengths and weakness identification

• Project management process

— Administering

— Assessing and testing (quality control)

— Communications

— Controlling through project management and IS tools

— Designing and developing

— Interrelationship dynamics

— Meetings

— Planning

— Presentations

— Project management office

— Project simulation

— Resource management

— Time management

SHORT LIST OF MANAGEMENT SKILLS AND TECHNIQUES

This book attempts to cover a number of management skills and techniques—perhaps some too briefly and others too exhaustively. This list of the management skills and techniques are viable to IT project management in many industries.

- Change-management techniques

- Coaching skills

- Conducting effective meetings

- Counseling skills

- Customer relationship skills

- Delegating

- Developing performance management systems and standards

- Employee career pathing

- Employee compensating

- Employee developing

- Employee empowering

- Employee self-managing

- Employee self-motivating

- Employee training
- Gender awareness
- Interviewing
- Leadership styles
- Listening skills
- Management audits
- Performance analysis
- Performance appraisals
- Presentation skills
- Selecting personnel
- Speaking skills
- Stress management
- Team building
- Time management
- Writing skills

OUTLINE FOR A PROJECT MANAGEMENT PROGRAM

As you expand your horizons, you must constantly develop new skills. IT project management is an environment that requires you to expand your horizons—in some cases very rapidly—because you have to see your functions through the eyes of those who may have a very limited knowledge of IT. You have to work with support functions such as documentation, training, human resources, and finance. These challenges can lead you to greater responsibilities and better awareness of the revolution in both technology and management practices.

These challenges include the following:

- Adjusting leadership style to the situation
- Communicating effectively
- Competitive challenge
- Comprehending organizational behavior which might be expressed as culture
- Comprehending personal and team behavior
- Creating commitment
- Creating motivation
- Delegating authority
- Developing a practical mission statement
- Developing high performance
- Empowerment
- Encouraging a common goal
- Generating creativity
- Identifying stakeholder expectations
- Identifying your own attitude and willingness to delegate and empower
- Improving teamwork
- Increasing technological complexity
- Leadership balance
- Leadership role requirements
- Managing differences in others to achieve constructive goals
- Meeting rising quality standards
- Resolving conflict

- Responding to rapid innovation
- Satisfying customer demands
- Strategic, tactical, and operational leadership role
- Vision generation

The above list might be formulated into these five goals to strategic leadership:

1. Defining the project's strategic goals, mission, standards, and policies
2. Identifying the process components that create value for the project customers
   — Who and what adds value to the process
   — Internal stakeholders and their roles
   — Demystifying the project process
3. Focusing on the essential competencies and capabilities (that is, skills) to achieve the project goals most effectively and efficiently
4. Establishing higher standards through benchmarking
5. Inspiring performance

IDEAL MANAGER OVERVIEW

Perhaps an easy statement is to say that an ideal manager uses common sense in all situations, but if there were such a thing as common sense, then we would all be acting on the same page. It might be that an ideal manager is using a set of common skills in an uncommon manner.

The first problem might occur when you start to manage your first project. You may not actually consider the required skills as "management" because you do not recognize them. Things go wrong not because you are stupid, but only because you have never considered the implications of the action. Managing is pausing to ask yourself the right questions so that you can provide the answers using the most effective skill or techniques.

Being a project manager for the first time and being a functional manager for the first time have different expectations. When you first become a manager, you can usually do what is expected of you, make honest mistakes. You are new at the job, so people will understand. However, as a first time project manager, the expectation is that you will use a set of skills to achieve the defined measurable project goals within budget and on time and with available resources. Life can be tough!

The second problem might be that you think that because under your business clothes you wear a cape and bright red and blue tights, you have become a super hero—or is that SuperManager? You think that because you have become a project manager, you have gained control over the situation; you have not. Control is an illusion. Use of effective skills is reality.

You can change things. You can do things differently. You actually have the potential to make a huge impact on the way in which your project team works. You can mold the work environment. In a corporation, your options may be limited by the existing culture and policy. A special skill is required because of this beast; face directly into the main thrust of corporate policy, and make changes sideways. You bend rather than fight the system to work better within it. In a small company, the limits may be broader but they are still there.

Once you demonstrate your managing skills effectively, this action will be quickly recognized and nothing gains faster approval than success. Do not be startled by the surprise colleagues will show when you first get serious about managing well.

You may not see yourself as a David against the Goliath of other peoples' low expectations. One of the skills required of you is the capability to meet resistance to change. Your success lies in convincing your team that what you are doing can only do them good, and in convincing everyone else that it can do them no harm. The potential is that soon others might follow you; this includes upper management.

This book is a summary of or commentary on the skills required to be an ideal manager.

THREE FUNCTIONAL ROLES OF A PROJECT MANAGER

The project manager has three major functional roles based on the project process, the first set of management labels used in this book. These roles are:

- Planner

- Provider

- Protector

As planner, you must have a predefined measurable view of the project goals that can be logically modified by the technical inputs of the team. The foundation of planning is the use of standards and continuous benchmarking against these standards. Each team member works on a project incrementally, but you must consider the project as a whole. By thinking about the eventual consequences of different views, you must select the optimal path for the team and implement it.

By taking account of the needs not only of the next project but the project after that, you must ensure that work is not repeated nor problems tackled too late, and that the necessary resources are allocated and arranged. In a large corporation, you must work with other project managers on related projects to ensure that they all meet corporate goals.

A part of planning includes vision, standards, and enthusiasm. You must communicate to the team a vision of a future that is comprehensible; standards in that the team needs a unifying code of practices which supports and enhances cooperation; and enthusiasm in that it is the best way of making the work exciting. You should dare to do what you have decided to do and to do it with confidence, integrity, and pride.

One of the most cited labels of a successful manager is that of *visionary*. In the context of this book, being a visionary means having the skill set to achieve observable goals that will also have measurable results. It does not mean having clairvoyance. It is not looking into a crystal ball, but using a logical process to achieve goals effectively and efficiently, to minimize risk and maximize opportunities. It is a concrete and measurable focus for the team's activities, which should sustain motivation and should unite your team. This implies two things: You need to know where your team is heading and you need to communicate this direction (vision) to them.

Communicating a vision is not a simple action, but rather an action that brings the whole team, not just some of the team, to perceive your vision and to start to share it with you. The vision must be a guiding principle for the decisions and actions of your group. The basis of this vision must be a set of objective standards developed by the team and from external sources. The vision must not be nebulous, but measurable. This vision becomes the project statement. The statement should be achievable within a given time and with available resources. The book tends to focus on planning skills for a project of less than a year in duration. However, these skills are also applicable for extended projects of five years or longer. There are just more inherent challenges the longer the project is extended. Ultimately, for an IT manager, the skill sets discussed in this book are a part of the day-to-day work environment.

The scope of your vision depends on the level of the project in the management structure, and so does the time limit on your project statement. A new project manager needs a project that can be achieved within one or two years. The design and development of a new aircraft takes far longer than this time, but the project planning skills have to be there. For example, if your team is in code design, your statement might be to automate the test procedures by the next product release to a specified level. You have a specific goal and a specific time to accomplish the project. You cannot have a statement that simply says "automate test procedures." This is a plan built on a very sandy beach with the high tide rapidly coming in.

As provider, you must have access to the information and materials that the team needs. It needs to be stated up front in writing by the appropriate upper level manager (strategic manager) that you have the authority or influence to acquire things which no one else on the team could. You may have to get from others data that they feel should not be shared with anyone, including you.

As a provider, you need to avoid pat answers to commonly asked questions. There is nothing so dull, for you and your team, as you pulling out the same answer to every situation. This type of action may lead to suspicion that you have not considered the question beyond a certain parameter. It is also not professional. Each situation and each person should be thought of as unique. You are the manager, you have to judge each situation with a fresh view, and you have to create the response.

Even if the established response seems suitable, you might still try something different. This is Darwinism at the local level, survival of the best response. By trying variations on standard models, you evolve new and potentially fitter models. Poor answers die, while successful answers evolve. If one does hold with Darwinism, one can try "Ockham's Razor." A part of this rule is to explain an unknown phenomenon in terms of that which is already known.

The skill needed here is to recognize that the situation and the environment are continually changing. The rate of change is generally increasing with advancing technology, more so in IS than anywhere else. If you do not continually adapt to accommodate change, then the response to a question may no longer be appropriate. You could go the way of the dodo or the plethora of dinosaurs. Your extinction will be caused through stagnation and inertia. Upon the heels of stagnation and inertia come project failure and a demonstration that you are not a planner, provider, or protector.

By providing even the smallest of changes you can build and motivate your team. You show, through changes in such small things as answering commonly asked questions in a variety of ways, that you are actively working to help them work; then they will feel that their efforts are recognized. If you also include their ideas in changes and even in the responses, then they will feel themselves to be a valued part of the team. There probably will be increased productivity because of the generated enthusiasm of the team. The team will actually want to work better. The essential skill of a planner is this: Before you start any activity, you must stop and think about it. You need to ask at least the following questions:

- What is the objective?

- How can it be achieved in a timely way and with available resources?

- What are potential alternatives?

- Who needs to be involved?

- What will it cost in time, resources, and money?

- Is it necessary to complete the project goals?

When you have a plan you should ensure how your plan is to work. At the simplest level of project management you need to at least do the following:

- You must find ways of monitoring your progress.

- You must have a set of objective standards for benchmarking.

- You must establish milestone dates for reviewing project status.

- You must establish methods for doing activities.

- You should decide why project meetings are to be held.

- You need to determine how ideas could best be generated.

- You need to comprehend there is no right or wrong way to do something unless it is of course just to sit at your desk and look blankly out the window.

- You need to consider the types of questions that will assist you in getting at basic issues and customer concerns.

- As an IT manager, you need to consider how to overcome the fear of IT jargon with non-IT members of the team.

- You need to sit down and plan the strategy for your group.

- Recognize that most data is neither black nor white, but gray.

- Acknowledge that your plan represents no more than the best guess you can make in the current situation.

- Establish a process to incorporate the new, practical information you have gathered into the evolution of the plan.

- Above everything else, remember you are working mostly with estimates.

As protector, you must ensure for the team security from the intrusions of less enlightened managers. At any given moment, there can be short-term excitements, which can deflect the team from the important issues. One of many examples is the rumor of reorganization. You need to provide the team with a type of security blanket as to how the project's goals relate to corporate goals that will not be affected by any type of reorganization. You should be there to guard against these intrusions and to protect the team.

Protection is a start-to-finish project activity. Even at the beginning of a project, you are responsible for costing it both in money and time so that the project team is not given an impossible deadline. You must ensure that any team member's suggestion receives a fair hearing and that your team comprehends the implications. If someone in your team has a problem at work you have to deal with it.

As a protector, you have to know in advance the external events that may impact your team. There are essentially three types of information: what you hear, what you gather, and what you infer. You must listen in meetings and in the hallways to what people are saying. You must analyze the minutes of meetings, project reports, and e-mails. You sometimes need to infer, identify the implications of activities or do simulations that can lead to new conclusions as to the project's status.

Any type of information can be vital, usually at the most unexpected moment. Surveys have revealed that many decisive decisions are determined because of the existence of an established information system covering the relevant data. If you know the full information, you can quickly reach an informed decision. This activity is important to the team's protection.

If you do not keep your eyes and ears open you are failing in your role as protector to your team. If the strategic manager comes back from an important meeting, have a chat. There is no need to employ subterfuge; merely ask questions. If there are answers, you hear them; if there are none, you know to investigate elsewhere. To use this skill, you must have already used another skill—developing a positive relationship with the strategic manager. You might provide the manager with a different insight, which might result in the manager's gratitude and future confidence(s). Being a protector must be done or you will be unprepared; but do not let it become an obsession.

Gathering information is not enough on its own: You have to analyze the information and to identify implications. Your success is determined by how well you predict the next logical step from any changes you see. There are project management tools available to assist in what-if scenarios. Your scenarios should show the implications across all functions involved in the project. An obvious scenario is if there is minimal documentation on IT output such as code, what are the implications for the goals on training and documentation?

A variation on the what-if scenario is to ask, "What could go erroneously?" By identifying potential problems at the project's start, you will prevent many complications and compensate for many more potential risks. You need to set aside specific time to do this type of brainstorming. It should be at least once a week and especially prior to milestone meetings. This skill is called *contingency planning*. Thoughts should be put in your project diary on a regular basis. The times for this activity should be written into your activities calendar just like any other appointment or responsibility.

BEING A LEADER

This book recognizes the historical reality, that each "leader" one can name has had a completely different approach. They all seem to wear many hats, such as chief, shaman, general, and manager. However, they may all have two common traits—a good memory and the skill to talk to individuals even when speaking to a group.

You may have read Machiavelli, but you cannot follow his position and expect to survive as a project leader. Machiavelli did not advocate being a caring protector as a means of becoming a great leader but rather that a Prince ought to be happy with "a reputation for being cruel in order to keep his subjects unified and loyal." You do not have the power to execute, nor even to banish.

You may find your team has a high degree of sophistication in this complex world. You cannot effectively control through fear, so you must try another method. You must lead yourself as you would lead others. Perhaps it is better to be modest than flamboyant. Perhaps you need to emphasize the "you" more than the "I." If you are quiet and modest, fear not; all you need is to talk clearly to your team and they will hear you.

The great leaders (managers) are the ones who challenge complacency and who are prepared to lead their teams forward toward a personal vision. They are the ones who recognize risks, seize opportunities, and create a future that involves the whole team. Ultimately, they are the ones who stop to think where they want to go and then have the shameless audacity to set out. This book seeks to identify skills that you the reader might need to become a better project or functional IT manager, if not a great one. All of this means being labeled a *professional.*

Section 1

Management Levels and Styles

This section has two overviews, project management levels and management styles. Project management has three levels of managers, based on the military metaphor:

- Operational—does the work on a day-to-day basis

- Tactical—IT or project manager

- Strategic—manager responsible to corporate management for the project's results

A management style is a label for a set of skills a person uses or does not use. This section focuses on five styles that show up frequently in project or operational management. Remember a management style may not be a day-to-day affair, but a style for the situation.

In Chapter 1, you examine the functions and skills of a manager at three levels for a project: operational, tactical, and strategic. In addition, the implications of crossing from one level to another are discussed as well as how to assess people skills at each management level. The project environment is discussed because the significant activities of an IT group are projects that occur in the networking and Internet environments. IT service and maintenance may be perceived as taking more of an IT group's time, but these two activities usually flow out of prior projects.

Chapter 2 highlights management styles that have been labeled over the years in management books: Dictator, Boss, Indian Chief, Mentor, and Guru.

This chapter briefly highlights four management styles that are discussed in Chapters 11 through 14: Organizer, Negotiator, Facilitator, and Salesperson. In addition, you develop the skill to discern the importance of a management style, which is the use or the misuse of a particular skill set.

CHAPTER 1

Management Levels

Objectives: At the end of this chapter, you will be able to:

- Give simple definitions for being an operational, tactical, and strategic manager during an IT project.

- Distinguish six core skill sets of an operational manager during an IT project.

- Identify 70 skills that make up an operational manager's profile for an IT project.

- Distinguish 16 core skills of a tactical manager during an IT project.

- Identify 158 skills that make up a tactical (project) manager's profile for an IT project.

- Distinguish three core skills of a strategic manager, level 1, during an IT project.

- Identify 24 skills that make up a level 1 strategic manager's profile for an IT project.

- Distinguish three core skills of a strategic manager, level 2, during an IT project.

Robert Anton Wilson said, "Whatever you believe, imprisons you." Perhaps it would have been better to say, "Whatever you know, frees you." No matter the level of management or the style of management you use during an IT project, the emphasis should be on knowing rather than believing. A project is an organized set of tasks to accomplish a set of measurable goals within a specified time with a limited set of resources.

This chapter, as well as this book, tries to demonstrate the differences between knowledge and belief. There is a great difference between knowing a person will be a successful project manager and believing the person will be a successful project manager. Perhaps the basis of success among the three levels of management is this point.

An IT manager, whether in a day-to-day environment or as a project manager, could be considered a tactical manager. This management level defines tactics or objectives. The management level above tactical is strategic—the manager who defines policy or broad goals. The level below is operational, or the manager who handles specific tasks. Thus, an important general management skill is comprehending the responsibilities or expected actions that belong at each level.

It was pointed out to Socrates over the door of the Temple of Delphi was its motto: "Know yourself." First, know who you are, then know who other people are. Do not guess. Can guessing even be considered a skill?

Operational Management Skills

Bluntly, the operational managers are the "grunts" of project management. There may be a number of operational managers. They do the day-to-day project operations. There may also be a wide span of knowledge of IT because in a large corporation project there will be such diversity as human resources, training, and documentation on the team.

Obviously, the first set of skills an operational manager needs to have is the five basic management skills: plan, organize, communicate, validate, and implement. An issue for operational managers during an IT project is to use these skills to adhere to the defined measurable goals of the project. In addition, the functional policies of an operational manager may conflict with the project goals.

Another set of skills an operational manager needs is one to handle cultural diversity. This skill set includes the ability to:

- Define cultural distinctions among fellow colleagues.
- Use inter-cultural (corporate and societal) skills to manage and to be managed.
- Relate to work and management issues in an international context.

A third set of skills is needed to motivate the staff. These skills include the ability to:

- Develop a personal model for team and individual motivation.
- Develop creativity.
- Identify the relationship between employee and company culture that fosters employee motivation.
- Maintain employee motivation within a dynamic changing corporation.
- Use constructive criticism.

A fourth set of skills includes the skills for communication. A manager needs to:

- Build an effective communication tool-box (listen, question, make non-verbal communication match verbal communication).
- Comprehend the significance of effective communication skills in today's workplace.
- Differentiate between one-way and two-way communication.

Another skill set is the one for handling performance evaluations. The skill set includes the abilities to:

- Conduct a performance evaluation.
- Define job expectations and set clear goals.

- Prepare for each evaluation.
- Review the staff in a systematic method frequently during a project.
- Use a model for performance appraisal.
- Write a performance evaluation.

A final set of skills is general in nature. This broad set allows a manager to:

- Create an action plan and use it.
- Know rather than believe.
- Use effective resource management principles.
- Use effective time management principles.
- Use stress management.

OPERATIONAL MANAGER'S PROFILE FOR IT PROJECT MANAGEMENT

As the tactical manager, an operational manager would consider to what degree any of the following activities would be done to achieve success while minimizing risk. All these skills or actions need to be at least considered for any project.

PLANNING SKILLS

- Recognize that the creation of the scope plan and definition is a team effort.
- Remember the purpose of the project is customer satisfaction.
- Remember to set forth a realistic set of measurable responsibilities.

- Identify how you and your team can be most efficient and effective in achieving the defined project goals for the scope plan and definition in a timely and financially sound manner.

- Remember not to let your specialized concern, whether it be technical, training, documenting, or marketing, override listening to what the customer has to say.

- Identify technical issues or risks that may impact the activity plan.

MEETING SKILLS

- Come to meetings with support data for activities from each area.

- Attend all the meetings; do not send an alternate.

- Inform the team of the outcome of meetings in a positive manner.

IDENTIFICATION SKILLS

- Identify the implications of required skill levels.

- Identify training and documentation requirements.

- Identify standards and benchmarks that might impact project goals.

- Establish cost estimates.

- Prepare an operational sequence of activities.

- Identify the impact of parameters and constraints of project goals on operational effort.

RESOURCE MANAGEMENT SKILLS

- Balance project resources.

- Be able to justify the why and how a resource is going to be utilized.

- Consider customer needs in acquiring resources.

- Consider if there are alternatives.

- Develop a formula for the availability of people for your group.

- Emphasize the need for skills rather than headcount.

- Procure approved resources.

PROJECT SUPPORT MANAGEMENT SKILLS

- Support the tactical manager with justifications for the resource plan.

- Work with the tactical manager to identify resource links.

- Work within the constraints and assumptions of the scope plan in identifying resource requirements.

- Identify the people who are knowledgeable enough to do the time estimates.

- Notify the tactical manager if there is no one available to do certain time estimates.

TIME ESTIMATING SKILLS

- Use the criteria created by the project team for developing the time estimates.

- Limit padding; actually, you should do *no* padding.

- Review time estimates beginning with the smallest to the largest for signs of excess.

- Include time estimates for quality control and assurance.

- Look for "forgotten" activities that need time estimates such as meetings, training, and documenting.

- Review the inputs of the project management software used by the tactical manager for your operational area.

SCHEDULE MANAGEMENT SKILLS

- Communicate to your team their part in the schedule and the significance of their actions.

- Ensure that the schedule includes quality control and assurance for your operational area.

- Look for "forgotten" activities that need to be included in the schedule.

- Notify the tactical manager when a known slippage is going to happen to the schedule.

- Review the inputs of the project management software used by the tactical manager for any errors in the schedule for your operational area.

COST ESTIMATING SKILLS

- Identify the people who are knowledgeable enough to do the cost estimates.

- Include cost estimates for quality control and assurance.

- Limit padding; actually, you should do *no* padding. Use a contingency fund.

- Look for "forgotten" activities that need cost estimates such as training or documenting.

- Notify the tactical manager if there is no one available to do certain cost estimates.

- Review cost estimates beginning with the least amount to the largest for signs of excess.

- Review the inputs of the project management software used by the tactical manager for your area to check for any corrections.

- Use the criteria from the project team for developing the cost estimates.

- Be aware of the monthly budget constraints that affect your project efforts.

- Ensure reliable cost estimates.

- Ensure reliable resource estimates.

- Ensure reliable time estimates.

- Ensure that if your employees do time sheets, they reflect only the effort directed toward the project.

BUDGET MANAGEMENT SKILLS

- Inform the tactical manager as soon as possible of any budgetary issue.

- Review with the tactical manager the results from the project management software.

- When you have a budget that includes project spending, then you need to treat those items as a project item, not as a business item.

QUALITY CONTROL MANAGEMENT SKILLS

- Support the tactical manager to ensure there is an appropriate quality program for the project.

- Ensure the best technicians attend the peer reviews.

- Manage deliverables so they adhere to the configuration control mechanism.

- Report promptly on quality issues and resolutions.

- Support quality assurance and control in its function so that it will not be obtrusive on the day-to-day project operations.

- Identify policies, procedures, benchmarks, and standards that assist in minimizing performance errors during the planning, design, development, and implementation phases for your component of the project.

RISK MANAGEMENT SKILLS

- Support the project manager's efforts in risk management.

- Document risk issues in your area.

- Identify personnel in your area that can assist in minimizing performance errors.

- Assist the quality group in the analysis and evaluation of any identified risk in your operational area.

- Minimize the risks and support the tactical manager who is managing the risk's solutions.

- Ensure the documentation reflects the measurable goals of the project.

- Analyze the project's goals to detail their impacts on any IT legacy software and hardware.

CUSTOMER RELATIONS SKILLS

- Remember, you are not a spokesperson to the customers; that is the tactical manager's responsibility.

- You are not to make project changes that are based on personal conversations with the customer.

- You cannot commit project resources without the approval of the project manager or the team.

TACTICAL (PROJECT) MANAGEMENT SKILLS

The IT manager has come to the forefront as a project manager because of how IT technology crosses all functions of a corporation. Many IT projects are being generated because of the intense global competition that demands that a corporation exert greater pressure to deliver products and services into the market. The basic general goals of IT project management are the same as the corporation's in this instance. These goals include:

- Deliver quickly.

- Provide quality.

- Develop a trained support group.

- Provide an environment for effective customer support.

- Work within a tightly controlled budget.

One of the first skills of an IT project manager is to resolve how these goals can be achieved. The skill is of course the ability to do effective and efficient planning. A technique is to get answers to such questions as:

- How is a measurable goal to be achieved?

- What skills are needed?

- Are the required skills available when needed?

- What resources are required?

- What is the minimum time required to achieve the goal?

- Who is involved?

- What type of schedule is required to achieve the goal?

- What are the customer's specific expectations?

- What are the measurable justifications for the project?

- Is it possible to do the project and meet the customer's expectations?

These are ten of the questions that an effective IT project manager must address in order to initiate an IT project to support the corporate business requirements. The IT project manager must ensure that the team acquires the right skills and competencies beyond their functional roles to achieve customer expectations, quality project results, and be within schedule and budget.

The IT manager must balance the proven practical tools and techniques for managing a project with the reality of the people side. The people have to be considered as individuals and as a team. Since the book is devoted to the skill sets of an IT project manager, only a broad sweeping statement is made here under the principle of "be everything to everyone." Besides being the one who can walk on water, and the one who can create a vintage wine from water, one might also be:

- Boss

- Communicator

- Dictator

- Expert

- Facilitator

- Guru

- Indian Chief

- Mediator

- Mentor

- Negotiator

- Organizer

- Reviewer

- Salesperson

- Spokesperson

- Teacher

Each of the above has its own set of skills. Some skills cross sets. Some skill sets have negative connotations. Some areas of the project management process that have to be considered in using effective skills to achieve successful project management can be included in the above skill set labels in some form. A very short list is the following:

- Be customer oriented.
- Accept responsibility.
- Acknowledge national, corporate, and individual culture and values.
- Be people oriented.
- Comprehend the implications of organizational relationships.
- Delegate authority.
- Develop alliances.
- Develop budgets.
- Develop organizational relationships.
- Develop schedules.
- Exercise authority.
- Motivate an effective and efficient project team.
- Use resource management.
- Use time management.
- Work with process management.
- Work with team dynamics.

As you go through the list you might ask what does the skill of developing a budget have to do with people skills? When you develop a budget, you have to recognize the needs of both the team and the managers that the project budget affects. Sometimes these needs are more irrational than rational. How do you handle a senior manager who wants to cut the budget as one of the "goodies" just before retirement?

TACTICAL MANAGER'S PROFILE
FOR IT PROJECT MANAGEMENT

You would not do everything discussed below, but you would need to consider all the actions. You probably would do all the actions of general management; it is just a question of degree. For a very small project, you could state your measured objectives, schedule, and resource utilization in a few pages. In a large complex project, you could expect to have hundreds or even thousands of pages of project administrative documentation. To show the complexity of the job, here is a random list of 158 actions required of you during any project:

1. Do not rush.

2. Do not be pressured in planning.

3. Use historical data.

4. The only silly question is the unasked question.

5. You should focus on the customer's needs rather than on the technical needs.

6. Recognize that everything has equal value.

7. Remember the most important words in any project process, "client" or "customer."

8. Never seek understanding, only comprehension.

9. For a project contract you have to identify constraints, the baseline, the terms, valid considerations, schedule, budget, required reports, monitoring procedures (all the various control mechanisms), and the closet procedures (historical and financial).

10. Be prepared to run the meetings.

11. Assign resource dependencies (skills, equipment, and materials).

12. Construct a sequence of activities and their associated times, the basis for the schedule.

13. Define procurement requirements, that is, the need for outside resources.

14. Define project activity parameters and constraints based on the project goals.

15. Determine skill levels required for critical activities and groups of activities.

16. Develop cost estimates against an activity or a group of related activities.

17. Ensure that the operational managers bring to the table support activity data.

18. Establish a project organization structure that includes links between an activity and a person.

19. Establish benchmarks for handling project administrative paperwork, training, and documentation.

20. Have a comprehensive quality control policy with specific activities and a defined sequence of activities that requires the involvement of quality control throughout the project process.

21. Identify potential risks and opportunities.

22. Identify standards that may impact the project activities.

23. Link budget items with defined activities with customer needs.

24. Remember customer needs come before technical desires.

25. Write the activity plan using fully confirmed project activities.

26. Assist the operational managers in preparing documentation for procuring resources.

27. Assist the operational managers in identifying resource links.

28. Consider customer needs in acquiring resources.

29. Consider if there are alternatives.

30. Develop a formula for the availability of people.

31. Emphasize the need for skills rather than headcount.

32. Ensure that there are budget allocations to support resource requirements.

33. Ensure that there are criteria that establish resource needs.

34. Identify skills first by labor classification such as *programmer,* then by name.

35. Know why and how a resource is going to be utilized in the project.

36. Resolve capital spending issues.

37. Resolve issues of the availability of resources to meet the schedule.

38. Validate the need for any resource through a detailed analysis.

39. Work with operational managers to ensure a balancing of resources.

40. Work with the strategic manager to identify available resources.

41. Write the resource plan.

42. Ensure that there are criteria for defining time estimates.

43. Define the estimates against the project goals.

44. Define estimates to average capabilities.

45. Do not factor in overtime or possible part-time efforts.

46. Time estimates should be done if possible by the person who will do the activity.

47. Define the time measurements (hours, eight-hour days, or 20-day work months).

48. Collect all the estimates before doing a total overview.

49. Use technical support of vendors to determine any installation or configuration time estimates.

50. Establish a process where time estimating becomes more a science than an art.

51. Resolve a too-large total of time estimates for the project by beginning with the smallest and working to the largest.

52. Set daily project priorities to manage time estimate issues.

53. Analyze time estimates to see possible impacts on the skills, resources, and materials needed for the project.

54. Determine with the operational managers what risks might develop with changes to the time estimates.

55. Resolve time issues such as getting a required resource well in advance of the required date.

56. Use project management software to assist in evaluating time estimates.

57. Determine how time estimates impact costs (each operational area probably has its own cost per man-hour).

58. Determine how the budget cycle might impact the time estimates, especially those in the fourth quarter.

59. Include time estimates for quality control and assurance.

60. Determine how time estimates may impact acquisition of outside resources.

61. Document issues and discuss at meetings.

62. Look for "forgotten" activities that need time estimates such as meetings, training, and documenting.

63. Factor procurement requirements into appropriate time estimates.

64. Finish the time estimate process before attempting to do the scheduling process.

65. Align the schedule to the customer's expectations.

66. Analyze the schedule to see possible impacts on the skills, resources, and materials needed for the project.

67. Communicate with vendors if applicable on the status of the schedule.

68. Create the schedule against the project goals.

69. Define estimates to average capabilities.

70. Define the lag-lead time relationships.

71. Define the start-end time dependencies.

72. Determine how schedule is impacted by varying cost potentials.

73. Determine how the acquisition of outside resources affects the schedule.

74. Determine how the budget cycle might impact the schedule, especially in the fourth quarter.

75. Determine with the operational managers what risks might develop with the defined schedule.

76. Discuss with the procurement group your project requirements.

77. Do resource and time leveling.

78. Document assumptions and constraints for developing the schedule.

79. Document issues and discuss at meetings.

80. Ensure resource availability in accordance with the schedule.

81. Ensure that the schedule reflects realistically the training and documentation requirements.

82. Ensure that the quality control and assurance schedule is appropriate.

83. Look for "forgotten" activities that need to be in the schedule.

84. Set daily project priorities to manage the schedule.

85. Smooth the schedule through a balancing of activities, time, and resources.

86. Use project management software frequently to assist in evaluating the status of the schedule.

87. Use project management software to validate various potential scheduling scenarios.

88. Use the activities to determine the schedule, not the other way around.

89. Validate the schedule by getting everyone's concurrence.

90. Ensure that there are criteria for defining cost estimates.

91. Define the estimates against the project goals.

92. Define estimates to average capabilities.

93. Do not factor in potential changes in costs.

94. Cost estimates should be done if possible by the person who will do the activity.

95. Define the cost measurements (hours, eight-hour days, or 20-day work months).

96. Analyze cost estimates to see possible impacts on the skills, resources, and materials required for the project.

97. Collect all the cost estimates before doing a total.

98. Determine how cost estimates impact time estimates (each operational area probably has its own cost per hour).

99. Determine how cost estimates may impact acquisition of outside resources.

100. Determine how the budget cycle might impact the cost estimates, especially those in the fourth quarter.

101. Determine with the operational managers what risks might develop with changes to the cost estimates.

102. Document issues and discuss at meetings.

103. Establish a process where cost estimating becomes more a science than an art.

104. Factor procurement requirements into appropriate cost estimates.

105. Finish the cost-estimate process before attempting to do the budgeting process.

106. Include cost estimates for quality control and assurance.

107. Look for "forgotten" activities that need cost estimates such as training or documentation.

108. Resolve a too large total of cost estimates for the project beginning with the least amounts and work to the largest amounts.

109. Resolve cost issues well in advance of the "spending" date.

110. Set daily project priorities to manage cost-estimate issues.

111. Use project management software to assist in evaluating cost estimates.

112. Use technical support of vendors to define any installation or configuration cost estimates.

113. Be aware of events that affect monthly budget reports (especially validate time sheet inputs).

114. Be aware of the impact of each vendor's invoicing cycle (you spend in the second quarter, the vendor's invoice appears in the fourth quarter).

115. Ensure that cost estimates are correctly entered by category or subcategory (refine the cost estimates into as many budget items as possible).

116. Ensure that operational managers do monthly budget status reports.

117. Ensure reliable cost estimates.

118. Ensure reliable resource estimates.

119. Ensure reliable time estimates.

120. Ensure that predicted spending is reliably given by month (do not divide total by 12).

121. Ensure that you have a budget to manage project administration.

122. Hold a monthly meeting on budgetary issues.

123. Identify funding for contingencies such as emergency travel.

124. Identify capital costs.

125. Seek the lowest staff charges.

126. Seek to reduce extraordinary costs such as travel.

127. Use project management software to evaluate spending prior to any monthly budget report (assist in identifying possible input errors or omitted spending, late invoices).

128. Place quality planning at the top of the project agenda.

129. Ensure that there are significant time and cost estimates for:

    —Monitoring activities

    —Testing deliverables

    —Evaluating performance

    —Measuring performance

    —Correcting performance deviations, errors

130. Guarantee there are time estimates for peer reviews.

131. Have a configuration control mechanism.

132. Create an appropriate reporting system on quality issues.

133. Assure that quality issues stay at the deliverable level rather than being considered personal.

134. Have separate lines in the budget for quality assurance and control.

135. Have a location where all standard and any other quality-related documentation is available to all.

136. Discuss risk potentials at all scheduled meetings, as a fixed agenda item.

137. Identify people to correct and provide quick technical analysis of risks.

138. Identify people who can do evaluations of issues.

139. Ensure that risk management has time in the schedule to do a proper job.

140. Ensure that there is funding in the budget for risk management, distinctive from the quality assurance and control functions.

141. Ensure that there are skilled personnel to handle risk evaluations.

142. Ensure that there is a contingency fund to handle significant risk issues.

143. Ensure that there are criteria developed during the planning phase for identifying risks.

144. Be responsible for risk management.

145. Have a risk management program that involves external resources.

146. Identify any special equipment that may be required to do analyses of potential risk as determined during the analysis and evaluation of the project goals.

147. Establish measurable objectives, benchmarks, and performance standards.

148. Prepare for potential risks by using a risk analysis tool.

149. Document all risks.

150. Keep management informed of potential risks.

151. Present measurable recommendations for solutions to a risk to upper management.

152. Make sure management comprehends the consequences of a risk.

153. Keep a neutral position by never saying, "I told you so."

154. Develop executive summaries for a project.

155. Distinguish between the support and the administrative types of documents.

156. Recognize when a document should be closed and another continued.

157. Comprehend the implications on the legacy software and hardware of the IS network created by any project.

158. Be the spokesperson for the project.

STRATEGIC MANAGEMENT SKILLS—LEVEL 1

One issue is that senior managers tend to think they should not be involved in project management, or else they get *too* involved. The strategic manager as considered here is a senior manager or director. The level 2 strategic manager exists in a large corporation where there are multiple IT projects going on under various level 1 strategic managers. The strategic manager is either the functional manager responsible to an internal or external customer for the results of the project, or the IT manager's superior.

Before any project, the strategic manager needs to work with the potential IT project manager to determine if the project is viable. The two should play a serious twenty-question analysis to answer if it is possible to do the project on time, with the potential budget, with potential resources, and to weigh all of this against the customer's expectations. A part of this task is to ensure that the customer makes available a set of measurable expectations. It is legal for one to smile at this point.

The strategic manager needs to be able to delegate in writing sufficient authority to the project manager to get the job done. In addition, it is important for the strategic manager to acknowledge to the team the significance of the project goals to the corporate goals.

STRATEGIC MANAGER'S PROFILE FOR IT PROJECT MANAGEMENT

A strategic manager may not do everything discussed in this section, but the strategic manager should *consider* everything discussed. A strategic manager would not expect the use of Program Evaluation and Review Technique/ Critical Path Method (PERT/CPM) for any project except one of a complex nature with large numbers of resources involved; however, some type of Gantt chart would be expected. Besides these considerations, 24 tasks that have to be followed in any project are:

1. Attend the first meeting and state at a minimum the following:

   — The project supports certain corporate goals.

   — The tactical manager, IT system administrator, has full authority to manage this project to its conclusion.

   — Summarize the conclusions of the evaluation for starting the project based on the twenty questions of the pre-project survey.

2. Chair the project strategic reviews so a degree of objectivity can be achieved.

3. Review the resource requirements.

4. Support any procurement effort in a timely fashion.

5. Ensure the availability of knowledgeable people, including outside consultants to evaluate the time estimates.

6. Ensure that the project's time estimating process is consistent with other time estimating processes in the company.

7. Assist the tactical manager in resolving any divisional issues on time estimates for the project.

8. Recognize that the project schedule is a plan, not a commitment on the part of the project manager.

9. Ensure that the project's scheduling process is consistent with other scheduling processes in the company.

10. Assist the tactical manager in resolving any divisional issues on the schedule for the project.

11. Ensure the availability of knowledgeable people, including outside consultants, to evaluate the cost estimates.

12. Ensure that the project's cost estimating process is consistent with other cost estimating processes in the company.

13. Assist the tactical manager in resolving any divisional issues on cost estimates for the project.

14. Try to get from higher management an acceptance that the project budget is a separate management tool and should not be treated the same as the operational budgets are during quarterly reviews.

15. Ensure that there is effective quality assurance and control for the project.

16. Establish an appropriate battlefield for excellence. The four cornerstones of excellence are quality, a realistic schedule, a viable budget, and solid risk management.

17. Emphasize the effort to minimize errors, not fight fires.

18. Ensure that the tactical manager has adequate historical data and enough skilled people available to do sophisticated modeling if required.

19. Acknowledge risk analysis as a proper project management and control tool or technique.

20. Support the acquisition and use of risk analysis tools.

21. Use the executive project summaries to monitor project results.

22. Give directions as required to ensure that corporate policies are followed, such as making sure the project quality plan is consistent with the corporate one.

23. Ask about the impact of a project as to how it affects the capital budget.

24. Be the spokesperson for the corporation.

STRATEGIC MANAGEMENT SKILLS—LEVEL 2

What was said for the level 1 strategic manager applies here as appropriate to the IT project situation. In addition, the executive manager should know better than any of the other managers what pressures the dynamic workplace can place on the IT project. The executive manager needs to assist the IT project manager to successfully operate in a flattened organizational structure, leveraging the available resources to achieve significant results.

The executive manager needs to use effective leadership to define and articulate the strategic vision of the company, contribute to the building of an innovative organizational culture and working climate, and make goals meaningful and understandable. The manager needs to establish and embed core values. In addition, there is the need to use mission, vision, and value statements as energizing forces, and to encourage creativity and intelligent risk-taking. The label for the level 2 strategic manager is "Energizer."

One of the areas where the skill sets of an executive manager can impact an IT project is the one that leads to improved performance. The level 2 strategic manager can assist the IT project manager to:

- Coach to build skills and stretch performance

- Develop networks and partnerships to enhance performance

- Identify and remove the obstacles to high performance

- Motivate through empowerment

Another area where this manager type can assist the IT project manager is in change management. This skill set includes the ability to:

- Anticipate the need for change

- Create the conditions for sustainable change

- Diagnose and determine ways to overcome resistance to change

ON THE CD-ROM

1. 01Whyqts.doc—Why am I at the level I am?

2. 01Overview.ppt—Chapter Overview

3. 01SOverview.ppt—Strategic Manager's Responsibilities

4. 01TOverview.ppt—Tactical Manager's Responsibilities

5. 01OOverview.ppt—Operational Managers' Responsibilities

CHAPTER 2

Management Styles

Objectives: At the end of this chapter, you will be able to:

- Make an assessment and discernment of various management skill sets.

- Identify 12 core skills that might be used in any management style.

- Give an example of when you would use the dictator manager skill set.

- Give an example of when you would use the boss manager skill set.

- Give an example of when you would use the Indian chief manager skill set.

- Give an example of when you would use the mentor manager skill set.

- Give an example of when you would use the guru manager skill set.

- List 10 questions that affect you as an organizer and your use of 12 core skills.

- List 12 questions that affect you as a negotiator and your use of 12 core skills.

- List eight questions that affect you as a facilitator and your use of 12 core skills.

- List 10 questions that affect you as a salesperson and your use of 12 core skills.

- Identify nine impacts on your people-management skills.

You should not consider being a certain type of manager and using its associated set of skills on a permanent basis. However, it is possible for you to have a dominant type and in the eyes of some people, perhaps you only have one type. In reality, you may move from one type to another in a given meeting or conversation—intentionally or unintentionally. A purpose of the book is to show that you should make a movement intentionally to achieve the most effective and efficient action possible.

A question that can be raised is "Do IT managers tend toward one or certain types of skill sets because of the nature of IT?" Perhaps you can answer this question by the time you have finished reading this book.

The ability to influence is often more complex than you might recognize. Changes in the working environment have resulted in an increased need for good influencing skills. The impact of the skill of influencing is in at least five management types in this chapter and even more throughout the book.

As an IT manager you have to work more across functions, lines, and units than most other functional managers. Very few complex IT projects are done only within an IT group. Even when true, such a project involves in some way certain support groups such as training or documentation. You must be able to influence your peers and superiors in other groups, without necessarily having line authority. Even with line authority, you have to influence effectively.

As an IT project manager, you have to work proactively, because you are responsible for following the process through from start to end and perhaps even beyond. You are under heavy pressure to perform, often having to do more with less. The less can be less time, fewer resources, or even a lack of technical or limited personal skills. Stakeholder management and networking take time, effort, and the wearing of many different management hats, but they are an essential component of being an IT project manager.

In addition, you have to build support across the corporation or company for your project. You have to be able to organize (Chapter 10), to negotiate (Chapter 11), to facilitate (Chapter 12), and to sell (Chapter 13). You have to have many different skill sets; all are vital for high performance.

One test of management skills occurs when managing for the remote environment. Remote does not necessarily mean being in widely dispersed geographical locations; one can be in one city and in different locations. What if the administrative headquarters of the corporation is in one building, the IS function is several blocks away, and various support functions are located in another building? Are there "culture" differences from one building to the next?

The skills of remote management are essential in an environment where individuals, teams, and organizations can be separated by distance, culture, and time. You are required to manage what is being called a "flexible workforce" of people who operate with independence and agility.

ASSESSMENT AND DISCERNMENT OF MANAGEMENT STYLES

Your managerial success and effectiveness are connected with the subjective judgment or perception that project stakeholders have of you, and of course project success. A management style is a set of skills used by you to attempt to create a positive stakeholder perception. The general view of an outstanding project manager presumes that you can influence people to be productive. During a project you need to have scheduled time to do an objective analysis of your influencing capacities, and the way other people see you is crucial.

The following skills are used or not used in a given management style. In addition, the degree to which a skill is used varies. The list is not comprehensive; for example, as is shown in Chapters 16 through 18, the communicating skill can be divided into written, oral, and presentations (which is a combination of written and oral). Before reading further you might take each skill and perhaps ask questions such as:

- When do I listen?

- Why do I listen?

- How do I listen?
- Where do I listen?
- What do I listen to?

The 12 skills below are a starting point for doing a skill assessment and discernment:

- Asserting yourself
- Communicating
- Facing crisis
- Giving and receiving criticism
- Handling emotional stress
- Handling frustration and anger
- Handling time
- Leading
- Listening
- Perceiving and respecting other people's feelings
- Relating to project stakeholders
- Selling your ideas to project stakeholders

NOTE

In the following discussions on types of managers, there is only the briefest touch on each to give you just a *feel* of a management style for your tool kit of project management. Each style could have a lengthy chapter devoted to it rather than a few paragraphs.

You as a Dictator-Type Manager

Perhaps the motto of the dictator type is "I want, you do." A softer label is *authoritarian*. This manager is highly prescriptive. Communication, whether written or oral, is probably in a terse manner. The project goals are important rather than the needs of the stakeholder. Overtime is an expected way of life.

The dictator might answer the five example questions as follows:

- When do I listen? I listen when my views are being approved or even more so when they are being disapproved.

- Why do I listen? I listen to ensure what I want done is done exactly.

- How do I listen? I listen closely for tones of rebellion.

- Where do I listen? I listen everywhere because rebels can be anywhere.

- What do I listen to? I listen to everything, but ignore ideas not a part of the goals.

Perhaps there is a bit of paranoia in this management style. As an IT project manager, do you think you would never use this style? There are times when this style might be used. It can be used as a "cold water" technique. What if an operational manager after talking to the customer decides without discussion with you to "enhance" the project output? When any measurable goals for a project, which you should have, are deviated from, there is always an impact. A change that causes one hour of additional work does not require the dictator; however, an additional month of work might. When you insist on everyone following measurable goals during the project process some stakeholders might perceive you as a dictator. The issue becomes a problem if you stay in this style at all times.

You as a Boss-Type Manager

This type of manager style has been acceptable until recently. There is an implication that many have forgotten that belongs to this manager, responsibility. Other ways to say *boss* include *foreman* or *forewoman, supervisor,* and *person in charge.* The negative connotation perhaps comes when the word was used as "master" during the period of slavery in this country. The word was used with the foreman, not the slave owner. You as an IT project manager use the 12 core skills in this style when you perceive your position as one of responsibility rather than the stakeholders as slaves. You define this type very early in the project process. You define your responsibilities when you get a statement of authority from the strategic manager. The statement carries within it an inherent set of responsibilities.

The boss with a sense of responsibility might answer the five example questions as follows:

- When do I listen? I listen closely when the conversation is about responsibilities.

- Why do I listen? I listen to ensure that everyone comprehends her or his responsibilities.

- How do I listen? I listen closely for concerns of doing the right thing.

- Where do I listen? I listen especially where people are discussing the carrying out of a project goal.

- What do I listen to? I listen to actions on completing project goals.

You may use this style subconsciously when you prepare a presentation for the strategic manager and you have a slide that shows the project require-ments and what has been achieved. In addition, you tend to emphasize your role over that of others. One method for showing you as "master" boss is to use extensively technical jargon in the presentation. This action will not get you any points with any project stakeholders except the "techie" types in your IT group.

You as an Indian Chief-Type Manager

Among many Native American tribes, there were two chiefs, peace and war. It was recognized by these tribes that while a leader may use the same set of skills, the situation required a different emphasis on the use of these skills. Is this important to you as a project manager? Yes. Is the IT project to enhance the bottom line of the corporation, or is it to resolve a crisis that impacts the corporation significantly? You can be the chief of time management or the chief of crisis management. How well do you handle stress? A chief is, in any case, the one principal authority who handles the practical or day-to-day issues in a specific environment. Can you be both types of chief? It is interesting that few tribes had one person who served as both. During a project to enhance the business, there may be a crisis—and for a short time in this case—the warrior might need to appear.

Perhaps the essential perception of the tribe toward the chief was that he was practical and knowledgeable of the situation. Thus, when the chief style appears, one needs to identify one's level of practicality and general knowledge of the implications of the project goals. Perhaps the chief appears every time you say, "Practice what I preach."

The chief with a sense of practicality and a focus on the situation might answer the five example questions as follows:

- When do I listen? I listen closely when the conversation is about the status of the project.

- Why do I listen? I listen to ensure that the project is where it should be according to the schedule.

- How do I listen? I listen closely for variations from the project plan.

- Where do I listen? I listen especially at planning and status meetings.

- What do I listen to? I listen to reports on project status.

YOU AS A MENTOR-TYPE MANAGER

The mentor-type manager has become popular in recent times. A mentor is a "teacher without a classroom" on the road of life. The mentor's stand is based on experience and the non-measurable characteristic of common sense or perhaps insight. A mentor could be an Indian chief in a teaching situation. The mentor type operates more at the individual level rather than the group level. The skill set thus has to be on the handling of face-to-face situations such as the job interview or more so during a review. As an IT project manager you need to use this with project stakeholders who have an issue in working within the project goals or comprehending the goals.

The mentor with a concern for clarifying an issue for an individual project stakeholder might answer the five example questions as follows:

- When do I listen? I listen when a person speaks about problems with the project process.

- Why do I listen? I listen to resolve an individual's issues on a project.

- How do I listen? I listen closely to give a response applicable to the individual's issue.

- Where do I listen? I listen to an individual in a private situation so an appropriate answer can be given to that individual.

- What do I listen to? I listen to an individual who is in need of my assistance to resolve a project issue.

You as a Guru-Type Manager

The guru-type manager is not a mentor. The two types work out of different modes. The guru works out of a spiritual mode or world of ideas, while the mentor is more concerned with the visual world. In a nonreligious sense, a guru is concerned with attitudes or perceptions. Answers the guru gives are more metaphorical than specific. The guru works in analogies and comparisons. Most IT project managers may not use this mode frequently. However, there is one time when this style is important: It is when you are talking to stakeholders who are not knowledgeable of IT jargon. You need to find ways to compare the IT jargon to a basis that the stakeholder comprehends. Notice the word *understands* is not used in the prior sentence because understanding is not measurable, while comprehending should be.

The guru with a concern for finding an analogy to bridge the comprehension of a technical concept for an individual project stakeholder might answer the five example questions as follows:

- How do I listen? I listen closely to determine an appropriate analogy to the stakeholder for IT jargon.

- What do I listen to? I listen to an individual who is in need of my assistance to bridge the stakeholder comprehension of IT jargon with the stakeholder's jargon.

- When do I listen? I listen when a person cannot comprehend IT jargon.

- Where do I listen? I listen anywhere there is confusion about IT jargon.

- Why do I listen? I listen because if a stakeholder cannot comprehend some IT jargon, the stakeholder might not give full support to the project goals.

OVERVIEW OF AN ORGANIZER

The organizer is discussed in more detail in Chapter 10. Being an organizer is one of four major roles you must play during a project under the more encompassing management style, planner. You are concerned with the structure of the project as to process, people, time, equipment, and materials. You will use the 12 skills given on page 34 to resolve at least the following questions of structure:

- How can the organizational forces change the organization's structure?

- How does the paper organization differ from the actual organization?

- What are the dynamics of an organization?

- What does it mean to organize?

- What is an organization?

- What type of team organization should exist?

- When do you organize a project team?

- Where does the customer fit into the project organization?

- Why does the organizational structure need to be defined?

- Why does the project need a quality control (place any other name here) group?

OVERVIEW OF A NEGOTIATOR

The negotiator is discussed in more detail in Chapter 11. Being a negotiator is a critical role in the project process. The use of skills that result in "win-win" situations is critical to achieving project goals. You will use the 12 skills given on page 34 to resolve at least the following questions of compromise:

- How do I define the issues?

- How do I define all the parties' requirements, needs, or wants?

- How do I establish an offense and a defense?

- How do I prepare to negotiate?

- How do I determine what can be traded?

- What are the dynamics of negotiating?

- What is communicated during a negotiation?

- What is negotiation?

- What is the difference between individual and group negotiations?

- When do I accept a "win-lose" situation, "lose-win" situation, or a "win-win" situation?

- When do I hold with your principles?

- Why should I negotiate on a given point?

OVERVIEW OF A FACILITATOR

The facilitator is discussed in more detail in Chapter 12. Being a facilitator is probably a role that you play every day of the project. To facilitate means to "oil the project's components to achieve effective and efficient results." The basic definition of facilitate is "to make easier."

You will use the 12 skills given on page 34 to make the project process move forward easily by answering the following questions:

- What is facilitating?

- Is facilitating more than touching and feeling?

- How do I create an environment for facilitating?

- How do I evaluate myself as a facilitator?

- How do I evaluate others as facilitators?

- What are the potential blocks to successful facilitation?

- How do I facilitate conflict resolutions?

- How do I handle the push and pull of interrelations?

OVERVIEW OF A SALESPERSON

The salesperson is discussed in more detail in Chapter 13. The fourth role you have to play during a project is salesperson. You say to yourself I am never a salesperson! Incorrect; you must sell your ideas to the team and you must sell the team's ideas to other project stakeholders. You will use the 12 skills given on page 34 to sell other stakeholders' ideas to each other to achieve project success by answering the following questions:

- Are there differences between an individual and a group sale?
- How do I develop a selling strategy?
- How do I handle resistance?
- How do I identify the complexity of selling my ideas?
- How do I prepare a sale to another stakeholder or to the team?
- What are the components of a sale?
- What does it mean to be a salesperson?
- What is selling?
- What is the importance of relationships to a sale?
- Why is selling a part of your day-to-day project experiences?

IMPACTS ON YOUR PEOPLE MANAGEMENT SKILLS

There are a number of impacts on your people management skills. One beneficial impact is doing a critical self-assessment, that is, "Know yourself." You need to examine your present skill set or sets on a frequent basis and refine and improve the skills as appropriate.

A second impact is the method or methods that you use to employ your skills. Your method will impact your interaction with others and the way they will interact with you. You need practice listening, communicating, and solving individual and group issues. At the same time, you need to be sensitive and assertive. In addition, you need to consider the method of how you work with individuals and with group dynamics.

A third impact of comprehending your skills toolbox is how it can improve your career. Comprehending your skill sets enable you in the long-term to handle your career effectively. In the short-term this knowledge enables you to manage an IT project effectively and efficiently for success.

A fourth impact of comprehending your skill sets is that it leads to self-promotion that includes such things as being more assertive with others, speaking out when appropriate, and arguing your position. Perhaps you will learn when it is appropriate to be patient and when to be methodical in project research.

A fifth impact of improved skill knowledge is that you become more decisive. This should enable you to develop competent project plans. In addition, you should be able to identify options, to assess their suitability, to choose the best option, and to put the option in action.

A sixth impact is that when you comprehend the implications of your skill set you should become more adaptable and flexible to changing or modifying your behavior in response to dynamic circumstances or the needs or wishes of project stakeholders. You should also be able to take on new challenges and responsibilities with minimal effort.

A seventh impact should be an improvement in your ability to hold discussions (negotiations) with others in order to reach a mutually satisfactory outcome. This includes putting forth your arguments without losing your temper, protecting your position, and knowing when to compromise.

An eighth impact is an improved networking capability. You should be able to establish rapport and a feeling of confidence when working with project stakeholders. The objective of this networking is getting everyone to work with everyone else and achieve goals in a minimum of time and expenditure of resources. This impact might be labeled *team management*.

The ninth impact is in the area of successful communications:

- Written—Expressing yourself well on paper, being persuasive, having a reasonable grasp of grammar and spelling, comprehending what the reader requires, and structuring your content to state what you desire.

- Oral—Using speech to express ideas, giving information, and getting your ideas across to another person.

- Presentation—Presenting both oral and written ideas or information to a group of people effectively, using visual aids confidently, and keeping their attention.

On the CD-ROM

1. 02SkillsList.doc—Skills Checklist

2. 02General.doc—General Self-Assessment

3. 02People.doc—Working with People Self-Assessment

4. 02Overview.ppt—Chapter Overview

Section 2

Managing Individuals

This section describes people skills required to manage individuals in contrast to teams as discussed in Section 3. The section looks at six situations where people skills are applied: hiring (selecting), motivating, developing creativity, controlling conflict, delegating authority, and reviewing performance.

In Chapter 3, you develop the skill to ask basic questions about other individuals for either being hired or selected for a project. One is shown why you do not say in an interview "Tell me about yourself."

In Chapter 4, you develop the skill to motivate people. It explains why intimidation is not a skill that results in motivation.

In Chapter 5, you develop the skill to encourage creativity in individuals that can enhance themselves and a project team. Creativity should not be considered a frightening activity of "thinking outside of the box."

In Chapter 6, you develop the skill to consider that the stated or viewed reason for a conflict is probably incorrect. This chapter focuses on the point that conflict management is the art of negotiation.

In Chapter 7, you develop the skill to delegate authority and responsibilities since project management is not an individual effort but a team effort.

In Chapter 8, you develop the skill to handle reviews for performance. It may be more difficult to give a review for a good performance than a bad performance.

CHAPTER 3

Hiring

Objectives: At the end of this chapter, you will be able to:

- Define the skill requirements for interviewing.

- Assess a resume.

- Write questions for an interview.

- State what is included in the interview process.

- Explain whether an interview should be a team effort.

- State the steps for doing a follow-up on an interview.

In this chapter, you develop the skill to ask basic questions about other individuals for being hired or selected for permanent employment, contract employment or a project. You are shown why you do not say in an interview "Tell me about yourself." In addition, one should remember that an interview might not be necessarily a moment in time, but a bottom-line result or consequence.

As an IT manager you have a distinct advantage over other functional managers in that you have so many job sites on the Internet where you can select resumes. Besides regional-oriented sites, you might look at these companies: Monster, BionicSearch, BrainBuzz, DiscoverJobs, HeadHunter, and ITClassifieds. Is this an advantage? Perhaps you still need the human resources department to do the filtering for you.

Fortunately (or unfortunately), according to statistics from the Bureau of Labor in recent years the fastest growing occupations impact IT hiring. The occupations are database administrator, computer engineer, and systems analyst. However, the secret may be finding the correct skill for the defined problem.

> **NOTE:**
>
> On the CD-ROM is an "Interviewing Self-Assessment" (03Interview.doc) that you should take prior to reading this chapter. An example of the self-assessment is also found in Chapter 23.

SKILL REQUIREMENTS FOR INTERVIEWING

Hiring is more than the basic interview, but all actions can be defined in the context of the interview. *Hiring* becomes the inclusive word for pre-interview activities, interview activities, and follow-up interview activities. The hiring or interviewing skill set thus can be divided into four broad categories:

- *Recruiting* is the process of seeking potential candidates for a position. This is usually handled by the human resources group; however, you have to define the parameters for the search.

- *Pre-interview skills* include reading a resume and developing questions for the interview.

- *Interview skills* are needed both as an individual and as a team member.

- *Follow-up skills* are more than having human resources send a letter.

Before you touch a resume, you need to do a few other things first. First, you need to write down the measurable requirements for the job. "I need a Java programmer" is not measurable. How many years of experience are required? What types of programming experiences are required? What level and types of Java knowledge are required? What other IT experiences are required? What do you expect the person to achieve within six months or one year after being hired? These five questions are only a beginning to thinking about the requirements. Do not forget the non-IT experiences.

The answers to the above questions can be based on an assessment of the person or persons that held the position previously. If a new position, how does this position relate to other positions in the IT group? Talk to your Java programmers about their expectations as to what is required for the job. This action is not only important for the hiring of staff, but also for hiring a new manager.

Second, you need to ask the major question, "Do I hire from inside or from outside the company?" Sometimes a corporation requires a job-opening announcement first for those within the corporation. You have to justify if you do not hire from within, so it is even more important to have a set of measurable requirements.

Sometimes you may think, "Why should I hire from within?" A change in position does not have to be a promotion. Someone with a high degree of motivation and an interest in IT may suit your long-term needs better than an applicant from outside. Unfortunately, one issue for an IT group is that it is usually under-30 males and white. This sometimes does limit the perceptions about corporate life. There are actually a number of nontechnical advantages for hiring from within:

- The person is familiar with and perhaps is adjusted to the corporate culture. This minimizes the risk of dissatisfaction.

- The person may perform at a higher level because of a boost in morale.

- The person speaks the "language" of a group other than IT and can translate the needs of the former group into the context of IT needs.

- You should get better evaluations of a person's performance than from the outside.

- Companies that hire from within seem to attract better outside applicants.

Third, you need to evaluate the role to be played within the IT organization. The first division is manager or staff. Is the manager administrative or operational? Is the staff to be a team leader, a "superstar," a player, "fresh blood," or a troubleshooter? Is the person to work with other departments or other functional groups?

Fourth, ask the question, "Does the position really have to be filled?" Has the purpose of the position changed? Can the position's functions be reallocated without too much additional effort on the staff? Will one person be as productive as two in this position?

Fifth, you need to consider the job's status. Should the status of the position stay the same, be downgraded, or be upgraded? Can the job be handled on a part-time basis? Can the job be shared? Finally, can this job be outsourced? Because you decide the job is to be outsourced does not mean you do not have to look at resumes. In fact, it is more critical because of the hourly rate you might have to pay.

Sixth, prepare a final job description. Take the answers from the above questions and your questions and then write a draft job description. Next, discuss this draft with a staff member of the human resources group. You are looking for a format that will get you a person you want. You need to ensure that you have the proper action verbs. If you are going to use human resources as a filter, you need to ensure that the human resources staff comprehends any technical requirements. I went for an interview where I was told it was for the development of a new telephone system and it actually was for a Y2K project manager's position. Was there confusion?

Seventh, check the job description for the following:

- Appropriate job title

- New changes because of the business

- Specific technical requirements (essential versus nice to have)

- Salary range (may be against corporate policy)

- Perks (usually found in a separate package)

- Vacation and special leave

- Overtime requirements

- Travel requirements

You might add to the specific technical requirements a "must have" or "desirable" label. You might have to send a desired candidate to training for a desirable requirement.

Eighth, determine how recruiting is to be done. This process may be out of your hands. You need to be aware of the possibilities and should ask the human resources staff what your role is. Some of the recruiting techniques include the following:

- Advertisement in the appropriate newspapers

- Internal job announcement

- Using recommendations

- Using agencies

- Using Internet job sites

The ninth and final step prior to the interview, is to prepare a filtering process. The process includes:

- Minimum criteria for any consideration

- Handling of telephone applications

- Handling of e-mail applications

- Handling of agency applications

- Preparing a standard rejection letter

- Preparing a letter for potential candidates for other areas

- Evaluating potential candidates (discussed in more detail in the next section)

- Creating a list of candidates

- Ensuring appropriate interviewers' availability

- Scheduling time and booking interview locations

Assessing a Resume

Before assessing a resume, remember it is a sales pitch. Each resume is different. To support the resume you will need to have consistency in information—a job application. A completed job application may answer questions about omissions in dates and employers.

It has been said that only thirty seconds is used to evaluate a resume. If this is so in your case, make good use of your thirty seconds. Have a checklist based on the answers developed to create the job description. First, you need to decide the number of check marks the resume must have before further consideration. Second, you must decide if certain items must have a check mark before further consideration.

Next, you need to look at the structure of the resume. If the resume is organized well, it perhaps demonstrates that the person's organizational skills are good. Remember, the person may have had the resume written by a professional. It is not recommended you necessarily ask the person directly, "Did you write your resume?" Are relevant skills noted? Does the resume show creativity? You need to look for inconsistencies (chronological, career moves, and times in jobs). Are specific accomplishments given rather than general accomplishments?

Other things you might look at are educational accomplishments, willingness to travel, and special work requirements. You need to work closely with human resources staff to look for any special corporate requirements or considerations.

Developing Questions for an Interview

Rule one is never ask in an interview "Tell me about yourself." To prevent this, you prepare before the interview. You have two sources for preparing the questions. The sources are the answers developed to write the job description and the person's resume.

If you have a specific problem to resolve when the person first comes to work for you, ask the applicant to state how the problem could be solved in general terms. There is a way around the one-hour interview. One could develop a series of take home questions to be returned in forty-eight hours. You could ask, "What role do you expect to play in the job?"

From the resume, you could generate a number of questions that clarify what is stated. You can ask:

- What are some specific results that you accomplished at job X?

- There seems to be confusion as to some dates on your resume, what is the meaning of these dates?

- Why did you move so many times during this period? (An obvious answer, the person worked for a consulting firm, but put down the companies for which work was done.)

- You seem to have changed your career direction at this point. Why?

You also want to develop a series of open questions, not closed ones that will only result in a "yes" or "no" answer. Some open questions you could ask are as follows:

- How do you think you can contribute to this company?

- What are some of your long-term goals?

- What are your strongest attributes?

- What did you like best about your prior positions?

- What do you consider the high point of your career to date?

- What do you think are your skills that you can contribute based on the job description?

- What experience do you have with problem solving (replace with any other skill)?

- Why do you want to change jobs?

You do not have to ask all these questions, you actually want to build on the responses of the interviewee. In addition, you might desire to make one of the questions negative such as asking for the low-point rather than the high-point in the interviewee's career. You need to see how the interviewee handles confrontation.

On the CD-ROM are Ten Interview Questions for IT Consultants (03CInterview.doc) and Example Interview Questions (03QInterview.doc). Examples of both are also found in Chapter 23.

> **NOTE:**
>
> There should be no questions developed that ask personal facts that are irrelevant to the job. For example, if you ask if the person can travel and the candidate says no, you should not ask why.

THE INTERVIEW PROCESS

This section looks at the one-on-one interview, while the next section looks at the team interview. If you do a series of one-on-one interviews for a single candidate, there should be a meeting prior to such interviews to discuss strategy. Some questions should be asked in common as a basis for evaluation.

First, on the arrival, stand and shake the hand of the interviewee. If there is a desk between the two of you and it is feasible, walk around the desk to do the handshaking. Try to put the interviewee at ease. Politely smile. Do not glare. If the source is close by, offer something to drink. Ensure that there are no interruptions!

Second, dress as you would normally. Be natural. Do not scare the interviewee. If the corporate culture is you should not dress in formal business attire, do not dress so. If the interviewee sees everyone dressed casually and you are not, there might be a question as to your place in the group even when your title is IT manager. I remember being interviewed and fifteen minutes or so into the interview, the interviewer said, "Perhaps in seven years you might have my position as director." Until that moment, I did not know his title. I got a very interesting flag as to his possible opinion about me. I got the job; unfortunately, in seven years I was not a director, only a second-level manager.

Third, evaluate the candidate by asking your prepared questions and their follow-ups. Place an emphasis on skills and experiences. You should be looking for organizational, analytical, communication, and decision-making skills. Your time is important, you should be decisive. Jot down notes. Focus on the candidate's answers.

Fourth, assess the candidate's personality. If the company has a team culture, you need to see if the person's preference is to work alone or as a team member. You are an ambassador of your company. While you are assessing the candidate, the candidate is assessing you, and thus, the company. You are looking for the degree of enthusiasm the candidate has.

Fifth, you need to control the interview. Do not let the candidate babble. If the candidate says, "I do not know the answer," move on to the next subject. Give supportive feedback, but do not be too enthusiastic so the candidate is misled, believing the job is in hand. Stay calm even if the candidate gets emotional.

Sixth, note the candidate's body language. Do not forget your own. Do not yawn. Remember, mirroring body language can generate rapport. Be careful in this area. This does not mean that if the candidate crosses his or her legs, you should also do so immediately. In addition, remember that the body language in one culture may not be the same in another. Look for signs of nervousness, evasiveness, and arrogance.

Seventh, close the interview by asking the candidate for questions. Be polite even if you decided this is not your candidate. Let the candidate know the approximate date when the candidate might receive the answer based on certain conditions. At the end, stand and shake the hand of the candidate and say, "Thank you for your time."

AN INTERVIEW AS A TEAM EFFORT

A team effort permits two views of the same statements. There has to be a pre-interview meeting to develop a strategy. If it is appropriate to the position, one interviewer asks the "hard" questions and the other interviewer asks the "soft" questions. You may need to see how the interviewee handles confrontation. All the skills of a one-on-one interview are valid. What the interviewers have to be careful of is not stepping on each other's toes. A simple nod may indicate for the one interviewer to take over the interview.

This type of interview with two or more interviewers gives support to your abilities as a manager. The candidate will probably work on a day-to-day situation with the other interviewers rather than you.

You might desire to have a standard interview form that the whole team fills out before there is a group discussion of the candidate. You will need a standard interview form if the candidate has multiple interviews.

THE INTERVIEW FOLLOW-UP

First, you need to analyze the interview as to fact, not as to bias. You may not like the gray hairs the person has, but then the person may have had them since the age of twenty.

Second, if you have a receptionist or secretary, ask for an opinion. A good secretary is probably more observant than you are.

Third, check your notes. How does the candidate match up against the resume? Remember some people are good at interviewing, but are not good on the job. This is not a cliché; it is the voice of experience.

Fourth, never compromise the essential requirements. You need to find an alternative or go searching again.

Fifth, if necessary call for a second interview. If you ask for a second interview, ensure that the candidate is still interested in the job. Have a specific purpose for the interview such as introducing members of the IT group that may be working in the same function or on the same project. Ask questions that go into more depth than the questions asked in the first interview.

Sixth, you need to work with human resources to make a final offer.

Seventh, you need to send personalized letters to other final candidates. You may have, sooner than you think, a position that one of them can fill.

ON THE CD-ROM

1. 03Overview.ppt—Chapter Overview

2. 03CInterview.doc—Ten Interview Questions for IS Consultants

3. 03Interview.doc—Interviewing Self-Assessment

4. 03JobSpec.xls—Job Specification

5. 03QInterview.doc—Example Interview Questions

CHAPTER 4

Motivation:
Recognition of Potentials

Objectives: At the end of this chapter, you will be able to:

- State a definition for motivation.
- State why group motivation begins with the IT manager.
- Identify general and business factors that can motivate.
- Answer the question "How do I motivate others?"
- Identify techniques for measuring the level of motivation.
- Identify skills required for managing motivation.
- Use a "no blame" system for improving motivation
- Use different motivational techniques for new and experienced staff.
- Identify six motivational guidelines.
- Identify seven techniques for motivating ambitious people.

NOTE:

As a part of this chapter, there is a Motivator Self-Assessment. It is found in Chapter 23 and on the CD-ROM as 04Motivate.doc. You should take the self-assessment prior to reading the chapter.

In this chapter, you develop the skill set to motivate people. It explains why intimidation is not a skill that results in motivation. Motivation is one skill set of high-performance organizations that cannot be omitted to change people. You need to ensure that your IT group has the right people in the right place at the right time. This means that you need to have people who can effectively coach, mentor, and counsel employees to develop and stretch their technical and interpersonal skills.

WHAT IS MOTIVATING?

Motivating is the skill set used to influence people's performances. As an IT manager you are seeking high-quality work and stretching expectations in both the technical and interpersonal environment. Motivation is simply the desire to act. The process should result in releasing the full potential of the group. The bottom line is that you want to reward successful work, but not threaten to punish unsuccessful work.

You say, "I do not know what motivates X." Just ask X. X will have an answer. You might be surprised that it is not necessarily very much. I have seen people who want or do not want an office by a window. The motivating influence might be flexible hours. Some people might desire to work in another IT team. Each of these is a slight movement up the career expectations ladder.

Motivation is a three-way street. You need to motivate your staff, your peers, and your superiors. The staff is obvious. By motivating peers, they may be able to support you in a time of need, such as in the negotiation of a project plan with a customer. Why should I motivate my manager? One reason is perhaps a better flow of information because of how your manager perceives you.

PERSONAL MOTIVATION TECHNIQUE

Motivation can be at the individual level, team level, or the personal level. Any motivational program in your IT group has to begin with you. If you do not appear to be motivated, no motivation program will be successful for your group. You do lead in this area by intentional or unintentional example. At the personal level you can:

- Analyze what really drives your career

- Examine future expectations and needs

- Have a continuous development plan

- Identify your portfolio of skills

- Manage effectively your skills portfolio

Self-motivation is long term. Manage your own personal motivation and encourage others to do the same. Discussing with others how you motivate yourself is better than putting up a sign that says, "Behind every dark cloud is the sun."

To manage your overall performance you need to do at least the following:

- Set high expectations for yourself and others

- Analyze basic tasks and lead others through them

- Choose and use the most appropriate coaching style

- Monitor your behavior and that of others

You need also to evaluate your progress by:

- Reviewing your drives, goals, and experiences

- Learning from your life experiences

- Highlighting your life's successes and failures

- Defining your future plans and needs

- Being aware of your skills to be a coach or a counselor

FACTORS THAT CAN MOTIVATE

Beyond considering your personal motivating process, you need to be aware of six factors or areas that relate to business motivation. These factors are:

- Advancement potentials
- Growth potentials
- Level of responsibility
- Project importance
- Recognition
- Work achievement

These factors assist in putting priorities on work and career values. You may ask, "Do I have to read a book or go to a class to become better aware of motivation?" No; look to the activities of a sports coach. This may be why motivational authors and speakers discuss being a coach. The skill set for motivation might be that of a successful coach. In your group, you should not be the only coach; you need assistants (your team leaders). For coaching, the skill set requires involvement in:

- Analyzing options
- Confronting alternatives
- Contacting and contracting
- Helping others learn from experiences
- Observing and listening

Some of this discussion is based on the ideas developed by Abraham Maslow in the 1940s. Many present-day motivational theories are based on Maslow's hierarchy of needs. From bottom to top the needs are:

- Physiological ("animal" needs)

- Safety

- Social

- Esteem

- Self-actualization (realizing individual potential)

You might be surprised how many people work out of the first three levels. However, to get a fully motivated team, you need to get them to function out of the top two levels.

General areas of motivating have been discussed. What about specific business areas where motivation is required? The following seven areas are important for building an integrated motivational program:

- Salary and benefits

- Working conditions

- Company policy

- Status

- Job security

- Supervision and autonomy

- Office life

Depending on your corporate culture, you may be able to influence salary and benefits. Unfortunately, it seems that in the IT arena, many employees look at the "perks" (especially stock options).

You can do more for working conditions when you think about it. You can determine if your group should have flexible hours and the criteria to have them. The criteria is important because if you state there are flexible hours only, then they are available for all. This fact may not be feasible for business reasons, thus the need for criteria.

A working condition can be so simple you might not think about it. A large corporation merged their sales and marketing group with the programming group. Since the sales group was made up of wear-the-tie types, in contrast to the casually dressed programmers, the first question asked by the programmers was "Can we still wear our shorts?" This is corporate cultural stress at its best. The sales group was wondering if their base salaries were going to be as good as the programmers'.

You need to keep your staff aware of corporate policies. A mischief-maker is the use of different colored badges. There are perhaps two valid reasons for having different colored badges, security and visitors or consultants.

A person's status can be very important to an individual. Be careful of naming a person as a project manager when the person is not a manager in the organization. "The title I have today should be my title tomorrow" is an attitude you need to consider when giving out titles. You need to remember that in the past the sanitary engineer was the garbage collector. Should a person with a degree in computer science have the title of engineer?

The attitude toward job security is changing. Yet, there is a need for a degree of confidence that the present project will be completed. You need to manage transitions and changes through:

- Helping others in transition-coping strategies

- Exploring your strategies for dealing with transitions and changes

- Recognizing and managing the stress impact of transitions and changes

- Developing techniques for being proactive in dealing with changes and transitions

- Developing better effective communication across cultures

The degree of supervision is based on your own degree of motivation and confidence in yourself. The issue of delegating authority is discussed in Chapter 7.

A positive office life requires a mutual personal and professional respect for each other. The big demotivator is diversity. Diversity is discussed in Chapter 12.

WHAT ARE SOME MOTIVATING TECHNIQUES?

There are five fundamental motivators:

- Achievement

- Recognition

- Job interest

- Responsibility

- Advancement

Achievement means reaching or exceeding a work objective. When you and the staff prepare their individual objectives for the year, you should never state an objective that includes "all" or "one hundred percent." If the objective says that the person must catch all bugs prior to group testing, how can the person exceed the goal? You should never have a percentage higher than eighty for defining success.

When a project or a major task is completed, there should be immediate public recognition. A standard letter from senior management six weeks after project completion does not motivate. I have been there. You probably have been there. You need to motivate senior management to recognize people quickly.

Job interest means putting a person in a position that they want. When people complain about work, it may mean the work brings no personal pleasure. Interest is a motivator. Do you watch on television a sport in which you have no interest? How long will you continue in a position that is not interesting?

When it comes to responsibility, you need to ask. Some people like to be players. Some people like a position that is risk-taking, self-directing, or decision-making.

People say they want to advance. You need to ask the reason. You then need to be honest about promotion prospects and a potential time frame. Some people will not hear you because they think they were ready yesterday. You need to find a situation for them that will not produce bottom-line damage that proves the correct position. You could be incorrect. The issue is not who is correct, but one of motivation.

TECHNIQUES FOR MEASURING THE LEVEL OF MOTIVATION

There are four techniques for measuring the level of motivation. All require outside assistance. The techniques are as follows:

- Attitude questionnaires

- Focus groups

- Opinion polls

- Unstructured interviews

Attitude questionnaires are usually sent to the staff's home addresses and the responses are returned to the outside company for analysis. You receive the results of the analysis without any names. This is a place for experts. You need to listen to the results and then act, but never sit back and relax.

A focus group uses an outside interviewer to discuss with one or more small groups company issues. Notice it is company issues not just group issues. You may get information on attitudes toward the company's salary policy or on other policies. Sometimes useful insight can be gained. Again, you will not be told what was said specifically by whom.

Opinion polls are attitude surveys. They could be used after a set of new reforms has been introduced. Perhaps the reforms are not really reforms.

Unstructured interviews by an outside interviewer may not seem practical, but it has been shown they can be as valid as questionnaires. The difficulty with this technique is the potential level of influence of the interviewer.

Managing Motivation

Depending on your corporate culture, there are any number of ways to motivate your staff. It is always important to comprehend the personalities that want to work in the IT environment. This starts with a look at your own personality. Now, what can any good manager do to motivate the staff? Here are eight answers:

- Acknowledge cultural differences.
- Avoid office politics.
- Be committed to the work.
- Be loyal to your staff, peers, and management.
- Be seen rather than assuming that you are seen.
- Collaborate with the staff.
- Place trust in your staff.
- Treat your staff as you expect to be treated.

Basis of Motivation is Communication

The importance of oral and written communication is discussed in Chapters 16 and 17. However, some of the techniques of any good communication program can be applied to motivation. Five methods for having effective motivational communication are:

- Bulletin boards
- E-mails
- Newsletters
- Selling techniques applied internally
- Telephones

HAVING A "NO BLAME" SYSTEM FOR IMPROVING MOTIVATION

It is a waste of time blaming people. The time should be spent correcting the problem. A part of establishing a "no blame" environment is to get in the habit of asking the following types of questions:

- What action was done incorrectly?

- When was the problem first identified?

- Where was the problem first identified?

- When were the first deviations identified?

- What standards and benchmarks were broken?

- How could this failure be prevented in the future?

Notice that none of these questions includes the word "who." In addition, you need to avoid "why" questions because this type of question can lead to a person or persons.

Beyond the habit of asking the above questions, you need to demonstrate that you accept risk taking. You need to explain to your staff what you mean by risk taking. It has to be rational and one needs to comprehend the consequences of a risk. A risk when it gets out of hand is action that is a detriment to the group.

MOTIVATION OF INDIVIDUALS

You have two levels of staff that have to be motivated somewhat differently, the new and the experienced. First, the techniques for new staff members include:

- Ensure that you personally welcome them aboard.

- Gently stretch their goals.

- Remember they have a personal life.
- Find ways to recognize them for their work.
- Find the appropriate motivating benefits.
- Find opportunities for growth.

Second, the techniques for experienced staff members include:

- Stretch their goals.
- Remember they have a personal life.
- Find ways to give more responsibilities.
- Find ways for promotion and career growth.
- Give appropriate annual bonuses.
- Place emphasis on job security.

At least annually, evaluate a job position for ways to enhance it. Enhance does not mean to place more burden on the individual.

NOTE:

The motivation of a group or team is discussed in Chapter 9.

MOTIVATIONAL GUIDELINES

These guidelines may seem to be clichés, but they represent the basic concepts of motivation:

- Motivation begins at home.
- Motivation means to get a person to move in the company not out of the company.

- Money is not a motivator, but a satisfier.

- A bonus based on productivity produces better motivation than a simple annual bonus.

- Things that motivate change from year to year. This year it may be flexible hours, but next year it might be profit sharing.

- Honesty is a great motivator.

PEOPLE NEED PRAISE

Everyone needs praise. How do you praise everyone? You need to find projects for those who think just getting along is okay so that when they succeed you can praise that accomplishment. You should only give praise for a specific accomplishment, not just for coming to work every day for a year.

Here are seven guidelines for praising:

- Do not be excessive in praising.

- Have a specific reason for giving praise.

- Praise in public.

- Be sincere in your praise.

- Listen to others when selecting someone for praise.

- Give an object of appreciation such as a certificate or plaque.

- Have an ongoing program to recognize good work.

TECHNIQUES FOR MOTIVATING AMBITIOUS PEOPLE

You have people who just want a job and then you have people who want your job. How do you handle the ambitious, especially when there is no opportunity for promotion? Here are seven techniques to motivate the ambitious without promotions:

- Give them special assignments that can enhance their career expectations.

- Give them important roles in major projects.

- Satisfy some of their financial desires with a compensation program.

- Have them assist you in doing annual budgetary planning. Salaries are your responsibility.

- Give them very special perks when possible.

- Permit them to be creative in enhancing the processes in the IT group.

- Find them serious mentors in areas of interests.

ON THE CD-ROM

1. 04Overview.ppt—Chapter Overview

2. 04Motivate.doc—Motivator Self-Assessment

3. 04ExMots.doc—Example Motivators

4. 04MotWkst.xls—Motivation Worksheet

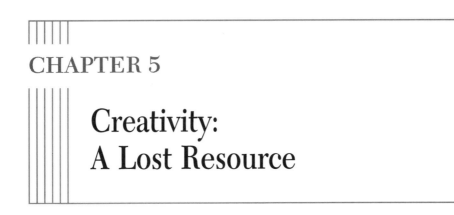

CHAPTER 5

Creativity:
A Lost Resource

Objectives: At the end of this chapter, you will be able to:

- State the importance of the use of creativity.

- Assess how you handle creativity.

- Identify four behavioral roadblocks to creativity.

- Identify a six-step process for managing problem solving.

- Identify six techniques for stimulating creativity.

- Identify three techniques for generating alternatives.

In this chapter, you develop the skill set to foster creativity in individuals who can enhance themselves and a team. Creativity should not be considered a frightening activity of "thinking outside of the box."

When dealing with creativity you need to consider these points. There are people who say they are programmers. There are people who are programmers. There are people who are good programmers. There are people who are great programmers. Moreover, on the rarest occasions there is an individual who may be a significant programmer; that is, a person who can change the field. Unfortunately, there are too many of the first type who think they are the last type.

NOTE:

Before reading the chapter, you should take the Decision Making Self-Assessment (05Decision.doc). It is found on the CD-ROM and in Chapter 23.

USING CREATIVITY

In a world of constant change, innovative, creative ideas can make the difference between success and failure, but only if you can manage those ideas. One of the basic management skills is to learn to harness the power of your ideas, and those of others, and put them to the right use at the right time.

Today's business environment is in constant turmoil; that is, management infrastructures are in dynamic change. New processes require new thinking such as the effective and efficient uses of the Internet and new business approaches that use cutting edge computer technology. Knowing how to develop practical ideas is a fundamental tool for your own success and your organization's future success.

Creativity in a business environment is not freewheeling, "Let's do it my way. Because of my youth and open mind, I know better." Creativity requires self-discipline in the context of the corporate mission statement and the IT group's operational measurable goals.

The concept of creativity has many variations that one should consider. Here is a short list of variants:

- Alternative
- Curiosity
- Experimentation
- Imagination

- Inquiry
- Insight
- Intuitive
- New approach
- Spontaneity

MANAGING CREATIVITY

To manage creativity you need to evaluate how you handle creativity in yourself and others. Below and on the next two pages are three brief assessments for routine problems, difficult problems, and fostering creativity in others. Within each statement is an implied skill. For each of the assessments, use the accompanying rating scale.

RATING SCALE

0   Never

1   Rarely

2   Occasionally

3   Frequently

4   Consistently

ROUTINE PROBLEMS

_____ 1. I can clearly and precisely define a problem.

_____ 2. I define the problem before looking for a solution.

_____ 3. I look for alternative solutions rather than one.

_____ 4. I consider the results and consequences of each solution.

_____ 5. I do research for data to achieve the most effective and efficient solution.

_____ 6. I use a problem-solving process rather than a hit-and-miss technique.

_____ 7. I revise a solution if it does not seem to be effective or efficient.

DIFFICULT PROBLEMS

_____ 1. I use the steps in solving a routine problem as a foundation for a further solution.

_____ 2. I work with more than one potential solution.

_____ 3. I try to be flexible with the use of potential solutions.

_____ 4. I look for a commonality or pattern among the potential solutions.

_____ 5. I look for the nature of the problem rather than considering an obvious view.

_____ 6. I consider both the irrational and rational possibilities of the problem.

_____ 7. I look for analogies to the problem for potential solutions.

_____ 8. I consider that my initial view may be completely incorrect.

_____ 9. I break the large down into smaller manageable parts.

_____ 10. I try to apply known problem-solving techniques to achieve a solution.

FOSTERING CREATIVITY IN OTHERS

____   1. I try to develop opportunities for employees to work without constraints.

____   2. I listen with an open mind to what employees have to say about solving a problem.

____   3. I use the strange position to challenge people who live "within the walls."

____   4. I use the principle that informed rule-breaking is a valid technique.

____   5. I use outsiders to stimulate ideas.

NOTE:

These assessments are found on the CD-ROM (05Creativity.doc). Anything below a 3 should be considered for improvement.

BASIC MANAGEMENT SKILLS FOR FOSTERING CREATIVITY

What are some of the basic management principles or skills for fostering creativity? There are at least six principles that are useful, including the following:

- Be an idea champion.
- Look for people to be idea mentors or facilitators.
- Hold people accountable.
- Accept devil's advocates.
- Have minority reports.
- Use both individuals and teams.

IMPLEMENTING CREATIVITY IDEAS

As an IT manager in a business environment you usually perceive creativity as problem solving. There are six basic steps for problem solving. The steps are as follows:

- Define the problem.

- Generate alternate solutions.

- Evaluate the alternatives.

- Select the logical solution.

- Implement the solution.

- Follow up on the solution.

Defining the problem means to separate the facts from the opinions, check all informational sources, state the problem in measurable terms, identify any standards that have to be broken, and identify stakeholders. You are seeking a correct solution not a right solution. You are working in a technical environment not necessarily a moral environment. As part of defining the problem, these issues might arise: lack of consensus, uncertainty as to the correct definition of the problem, and the problem is defined in terms of the solution.

Generating alternate solutions means to consider more than one idea prior to having a final solution, to have a broad participation for developing ideas, to develop solutions consistent with the corporate mission statement and with the IT operational objectives, to consider results (positives) and consequences (negatives), and to search for commonality or patterns among the solutions. Do not evaluate solutions before getting all the options on the table. When generating alternate solutions these issues may arise: desire to evaluate solutions before all are on the table, the first suggestion becomes the solution, past solutions are given more validity than new ones, and development of alternatives is difficult.

Evaluating the alternatives includes determining the solution that directly affects the defined problem most. You need to determine if you have the solution that gives the best results with the least consequences. Do not accept the first solution. The solution should perhaps be the most optimal rather than the most comprehensive. Remember that 20 percent of the work gives you 80 percent of the goal. The alternative selected should be stated explicitly. Some of the issues that might happen during the evaluation of alternatives include: gathering information is costly, there is limited information, people desire a satisfactory solution rather than an optimal solution, and people desire to implement a solution before there is a precise problem definition.

Implementing a solution only happens after the prior problem-solving steps have occurred. There should be feedback as to how well the implementation is occurring. Do not test only at the end of the implementation process. A part of the implementation process is to develop support and acceptance for the solution. When you go to implement a solution, a number of issues can arise—including resistance to change, length of time to implement the solution, and corporate politics.

Following up is on occasion ignored, but it is as critical to the process as any other step. You need both short-term and long-term data on the success of the solution. This type of data should be used in future problem-solving situations. The ultimate question is "Did the solution resolve the problem?"

As part of managing creativity, you must be able to identify behavioral roadblocks. Four of these roadblocks are the following:

- Commitment—Solving a problem in terms of the past

- Complacency—Doing rather than thinking

- Compression—Defining the problem in the narrowest terms possible

- Constancy—Defining the problem vertically without the possibility of alternatives

When facing commitment, you have a person who keeps saying, "Let us get on with the work." The commitment is negative in the sense that the person has decided as an individual the problem and the solution rather than any consideration of others. My way is right!

When facing complacency the person is probably in the nonthinking mode. One of the factors that may cause complacency is insecurity. The insecurity may be because the person is new to the group, or the problem in some manner challenges the person's position. Society does not support bad ideas, so some people will not speak up about the ideas they have.

When facing compression, you have a person who fails to consider new solutions. What we did in the past is good enough for today, is the position taken. The person is putting artificial boundaries on the problem and potential solutions. In addition, the person may not be able to distinguish the important from the unimportant.

When facing constancy, you have to open a person's restricted view of a problem to new perspectives. One might have to use analogies or metaphors. This type of person thinks since the Web site was done in HTML, any enhancement must be in HTML. There is no place for XML in solving the problem. To this person black is black. One would have a problem in saying black reflects no light.

TECHNIQUES FOR STIMULATING CREATIVITY

Creativity is in all of us. Here are six techniques for doing this type of stimulation:

- Make the common strange and make the strange common.

- Look at all sides of the problem (lateral thinking).

- Embellish the definition.

- Be flexible as to what you see and think.

- Turn the definition inside out.

- Unclutter your mind.

Literal thinking is to recognize that when you draw a line on a piece of paper, it has four sides. You usually only notice the top one. When the paper is thin reverse the paper and hold it up to a strong light. Do you see now the bottom of the line?

GENERATING ALTERNATIVES

How can I generate more alternatives? When a problem appears to only have one solution, you need to look again using a technique to stimulate creativity. Here are three specific techniques for this problem:

- Defer judgment through brainstorming.

- Expand the list of alternatives.

- Look for links in the unrelated.

ON THE CD-ROM

1. 05Overview.ppt—Chapter Overview

2. 05Creativity.doc—Three Assessments for Managing Creativity

3. 05Decision.doc—Decision Making Self-Assessment

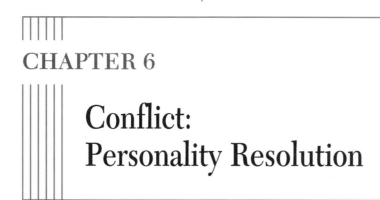

CHAPTER 6

Conflict:
Personality Resolution

Objectives: At the end of this chapter, you will be able to:

- State a definition of conflict.

- Give five examples of causes of conflicts.

- Answer the question, "How should I handle conflict?"

- State the differences between mediation and arbitration.

In this chapter, you develop the skills to consider that the stated or viewed reason for a conflict is probably incorrect. The chapter focuses on the point that conflict management is the art of negotiation, and the basis for most conflict is stress.

The basis of conflict management is the traditional principle: Conflict must be avoided. The question is, "Should all conflicts be avoided?" Perhaps you can have conflicts; they just have to be managed. Does the absence of conflict result in group atrophy?

NOTE:

Before reading this chapter, you should take the Handling Stress Self-Assessment (06Stress.doc) found on the CD-ROM and in Chapter 23.

DEFINITION OF CONFLICT

The essence of any conflict is what two or more people think is reality is actually two or more views of reality as it "ought to be." Perhaps all parties are incorrect. This is a reason for measurable objectives, standards, and benchmarks.

In some arguments the word *truth* is used instead of "the way I think it ought to be." You could be philosophical and ask, "What is truth?" It is quicker to answer that truth is what all parties agree on at a physical level of observation and at a logical level of abstraction. Truth is more an irrational agreement than a rational agreement. The skill set of conflict management requires you to comprehend the emotional viewpoints of your employees or project stakeholders to achieve success.

While the above definition gives emphasis to the conflict between individuals, there are actually five types of conflict. As an IT manager who has a mission to extend your group's efforts beyond your own group, you have to use your managerial skill set to work with all these conflict types:

- Intrapersonal (within a single individual such as death of a spouse)

- Interpersonal (between individuals)

- Intragroup (within a group, such as a group's functional direction)

- Intergroup (between groups)

- Interorganizational (between organizations)

An intraorganizational conflict is the same as an intragroup conflict except with more people. One can replace the word "group" with "team."

Unfortunately, many managers try to resolve intrapersonal conflicts, when it requires professionals in this area. An IT manager is a technical professional; people in human resources are people professionals. Have you been trained to handle or confront an individual's psychological defense mechanisms? An important skill is to acknowledge that others may have the skills to handle intrapersonal conflicts better than you. It takes more than the sending of flowers when one of your staff's spouse dies to resolve an intrapersonal conflict.

When it comes to managing interpersonal conflicts, you have to identify the real reason for the conflict, not the perceived one. The next section in the chapter gives example causes of possible conflicts. Remember that usually the underpinning cause is stress. What causes the stress?

When it comes to intragroup conflicts, one looks to the principles of team management. These principles are discussed in Chapter 9. Intragroup conflicts can develop quickly when there is no specific functional goal. The goal of writing code is not very specific. There needs to be a common set of norms or values held by the group to reduce stress.

Intergroup conflict is between two groups or teams such as programmers and nonprogrammers (task-focused issues). On a grander scale it could be the IT group and non-IT groups (relationship issues). There are at least four categories of intergroup conflict:

- Diversity (discussed in Chapter 12)
- Line-staff (creators of products versus service maintainers)
- Horizontal (peer-level conflicts)
- Vertical (different-level conflicts)

How do you manage intergroup conflicts? There are five potential modes of which the last is the most positive: sidestep the conflict (avoidance), win the conflict as the other side's interests (win-lose), permit the other side to win at your interests (lose-win), compromise, and collaboration. Collaboration is working together so both sides can be satisfied (win-win).

EXAMPLES OF CAUSES OF CONFLICTS

While stress is the basis of conflicts, conflicts manifest themselves in a number of ways. Here are five possibilities:

- Lack of rewards and promotions

- Misunderstanding over project objectives

- Organizational misunderstandings

- Resource competition

- Threats to job security

The causes, results, and consequences of group dynamics, which can be the basis for some conflicts, are discussed in Chapters 2, 9, and 12.

How Should I Handle Conflict?

One way to see how to manage conflict is to consider ways not to manage it. Unfortunately, when you look around you may see that your peers and perhaps one or two of the upper management use these methods:

- Demands the right answer

- Desires a short-term solution rather than a long-range solution

- Does not listen

- Is intolerant of ambiguity

- Looks at the general rather than the parts

- Rushes through to achieve the quickest solution

- Sees the side that confirms their biases

- Selects only certain information

- Uses a single approach to solving any problem

- Uses old habits to solve the new problems

Do these methods solve conflicts? No, they only increase the stress, thus the conflict. To handle conflict not only impacts personal development;

it impacts the bottom line of the business. The basic skill set of conflict management is to listen, be objective, solve the problem in an appropriate manner, plan, and generate new ideas.

In conflict management, you are searching for results, not consequences. You want to have justice, not judgment. Justice is a balance, not a one-sided opinion. You want to resolve stress, not be compassionate. Compassion is giving in to the irrational rather than looking for a rational business solution.

One way to consider conflict management is the use of one of three strategies: reactive, proactive, and meta-active. The reactive strategy is the strategy most commonly used. You look at the short-term situation and you look for a temporary coping solution. The proactive is long-term and you seek an initiative to negate the stress. The final strategy is a search for a permanent solution that includes creating a different environment for the person or persons of concern. You can easily see why the final strategy is the only valid one. The stress will return with either of the other two strategies.

One of the techniques of conflict management is to comprehend the sources of stress. The following ten categories of stress represent areas of bad time management, personal conflicts, societal stress, and emotional stress:

- Action conflict

- Anxiety (when fear, it is numbing)

- Business change

- Cultural change (death of a spouse is the big one)

- Issue conflict

- Loss of control

- Role conflict

- Unfavorable working conditions

- Unpleasant expectations (did not get the raise expected)

- Work overload (overtime is only a manifestation)

You can see that outside business situations can easily spill into the business when you have to manage a conflict that, on first appearance, appears to be a business issue. One of the reasons for being objective is you have to look for the less than obvious. You have to work harder when you are closer to one of the parties of the conflict. You have to put technical competence on the back burner. The consequences of the conflict can spill beyond the involved parties.

There are four broad techniques for managing these categories of stress. First, consider how you can implement effective and efficient personal and business time management techniques for the parties involved in the conflict. Second, consider how a redesign of the work environment might assist as a solution. Third, determine what interpersonal behavioral skills have to be applied. Fourth, look for small wins and a win-win solution. Whatever the technique used, you must search for the permanent solution.

MEDIATION AND ARBITRATION

There are two types of resolutions when you use these techniques, mediation and arbitration. You are either the mediator or arbitrator. As mediator, you seek to have the parties resolve their issues. Both parties must have a clear comprehension of the goals of the mediation. As arbitrator, you listen to both parties and then make an objective decision. Mediation is obviously better than arbitration because you become the outside force that has to resolve the issue.

In mediation, you need to narrow down the areas of disagreement and to widen the areas of agreement. Have one person give a statement of position. Have the other person repeat the statement as heard. Clarify differences in views. Repeat the process with the second person. You should then summarize both the agreement and disagreement areas. You need the parties to determine how they can resolve the disagreements. You keep repeating this process until there is a resolution.

In arbitration, you have to treat the parties as adults even if they act as children. Based on the gathered facts and an evaluation of the facts, you seek an alternative that is a compromise. You then make a decision and explain to the parties your reasoning before implementing the solution.

ON THE CD-ROM

1. 06Overview.ppt—Chapter Overview
2. 06Stress.doc—Handling Stress Self-Assessment

CHAPTER 7

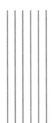

Authority and Responsibility: Delegation through Trust

Objectives: At the end of this chapter, you will be able to:

- Answer the question, "What is delegation of authority?"
- State reasons for delegating authority.
- Identify requirements for success when you delegate.
- Answer the question, "When should you delegate authority?"
- Answer the question, "How should you delegate authority?"
- Decide what tasks to delegate.

NOTE:

As a part of the chapter, there is a Delegating Skills Self-Assessment. It is found in Chapter 23 and on the CD-ROM as 07Delegate.doc.

In this chapter, you develop the skill set to delegate authority and responsibilities since management is not an individual effort, but a team effort. Delegation is a skill of which we have all heard—but which few comprehend. It might be used as an excuse for dumping failure onto the shoulders of subordinates; then you really have no authority. It can be used as a dynamic tool for motivating and training your staff to realize their full potential.

What is Delegation of Authority?

Everyone knows about delegation. Few actually comprehend what it is. Delegation is a foundation of a management style that allows your staff an opportunity to use and develop their skills and knowledge to the full potential. Without delegation, you lose their full value.

Delegation is primarily a matter of trust, permitting others to use your authority. This means that they can act and initiate independently; and that they assume responsibility with you for certain tasks. You still have responsibility even when you delegate your authority. You cannot delegate responsibility. If something goes awry, you remain responsible since you are the manager. The skill is to delegate in such a way that things are done, but do not go too badly. To keep things from going awry you should:

- Define the task.
- Monitor the status of the task.
- Encourage the individual handling the task.
- Coach when the task seems to be going awry.
- Review the task when appropriate.

Remember the task can be small or very large. A fundamental principle of delegation is to begin with the small and evolve to the large.

Objectives of Delegation of Authority

There are a number of reasons for delegating authority from personal to situational. Here are four general reasons:

- Reduce your stress

- Give you more time to manage the high-level events

- Give an opportunity for motivation

- Acknowledgment that others can do a task that you could do better

Here are ten specific reasons for delegating authority:

- Improve organizational effectiveness

- Maximize organizational strengths

- Minimize organizational weaknesses

- Recognize employees' capabilities and skills

- Utilize people resources effectively

- Use empowerment

- Shorten the decision-making process

- Match assignments to talents

- Cause people to solve their own problems

- Build a cadre of potential team leaders or managers

The objective of delegation is to get the job done by someone else. Delegation is not just the simple tasks of developing a set of instructions, but also the decision-making. Changes should be made depending on new data.

With delegation, your staff has the authority to react to situations without referring back to you on an hourly or daily basis. Delegation can be very specific or very open, such as coding one function on one feature or coding many functions on a feature that is necessary to meet the customer's goals.

To make certain someone else can do the task for you, you must ensure that the individual:

- Knows what you require

- Has sufficient authority to achieve your requirements

- Knows how to do it

It is all communication, communication, and communication.

What are the environmental requirements to achieve success when you delegate authority? Here are sixteen requirements:

1. You have a system to enable the flow of information. Your staff needs to know that the same information available to you is available to them if you delegate a job.

2. You have a decision-making process.

3. You have an environment where risk-taking is possible.

4. You have a system where creativity is acknowledged.

5. You have demonstrated loyalty to your staff.

6. You use the power of computerized information distribution to facilitate the rapid dissemination of information.

7. You have an effective quality control and assurance process.

8. You have the known expectation that your staff will apply the same criteria as you would yourself.

9. You ensure that the staff member does not feel the task must be done alone. There is always your support.

10. You do not delegate a task that cannot possibly be achieved by the staff member.

11. You believe that delegation is a concrete technique rather than an abstract technique.

12. You need to demonstrate that you feel confident in the staff member's skills and abilities.

13. You establish a schedule for regular reviews, thus constraining availability.

14. You establish benchmarks and standards for success.

15. You discuss potential solutions, not personal capabilities.

16. When there are problems, you speak in specific terms.

DECIDING WHAT TASKS TO DELEGATE

There is always the question of which tasks to delegate and which tasks to do yourself. You must take a long-term view on this. You should delegate as much as possible to develop your staff.

The beginning point is to list the activities you used to do before you were promoted. You were once a junior staff member. What opportunities were given to you so you could grow? What opportunities did you want so you could grow in your career?

Perhaps the easiest tasks you can delegate are the ones in which you have experience. You can explain these tasks most clearly to others so they can take over these tasks. Your experience becomes the basis for the next generation to learn.

Tasks in which your staff members have more experience must be delegated to them. This does not mean that you no longer have responsibility because they are experts, but it does mean that the default decision-making should be theirs. They do need to know your criteria for making decisions.

In terms of motivation for your staff, you should distribute both the mundane and exciting tasks as evenly as possible. In especially boring tasks, you should be careful to delegate not only the performance of the task but also its ownership. You should be looking for innovation. The point is that you need to explain that the task may be changed, developed, or upgraded if necessary or desirable.

There are managerial functions that you should never delegate. These are the personal and personnel ones. These functions include motivation, organization, overall budgetary tasks, training, team building, organization, praising, reprimanding, performance reviews, and promoting. You have a responsibility to represent and to develop the effectiveness of your group. These tasks can fill up your available time. Delegation is an opportunity for your own career growth.

On the CD-ROM

1. 07Overview.ppt—Chapter Overview

2. 07Delegate.doc—Delegating Skills Self-Assessment

3. 07Delegate.xls—Delegation Worksheet

CHAPTER 8

The Review: Highlight Success, Shadow Failure

Objectives: At the end of this chapter, you will be able to:

- Answer the question, "What should a performance review accomplish?"
- Use a self-assessment to prepare for a performance review.
- Identify a five-step performance review process.
- List the skills required for a performance review cycle.
- Identify effective phrases for a performance review.

In this chapter, you develop the skills to handle reviews for performance. It may be more difficult to give a review for a good performance than a bad performance. However, an IT manager probably has something very few other managers have: extensive performance system data that can be used in developing measurable objectives for a review.

> **NOTE:**
>
> Besides the Review Skills Self-Assessment in this chapter you should take the Feedback Skills Self-Assessment (08Feedback.doc) found in Chapter 23 and on the CD-ROM.

What Should a Performance Review Accomplish?

A performance review should be an objective appraisal against prior accepted measurable and achievable objectives that give an opportunity to exceed. An objective that includes "all" or "100%" does not give an opportunity to exceed, only the opportunity to fail. The review should be the culmination of a series of discussions.

> **NOTE:**
>
> Whenever the word *review* appears by itself in the chapter, it always means *performance review*.

Self-Assessment as a Foundation for a Review

How can a self-assessment help review another person? Your actions and opinions do impact the outcome. For the statements below, rate yourself on the skills:

RATING SCALE

0   Never

1   Rarely

2   Occasionally

3   Frequently

4   Consistently

____   1. I accept feedback.

____   2. I seek to find out from others the performance strengths and weaknesses of the person being reviewed.

____ 3. I have techniques to handle ambiguous situations.

____ 4. I am conscious of potentially contentious areas.

____ 5. I know I have to control my temper in delicate situations.

____ 6. I seek to find the positive in the negative.

____ 7. I manage for success, not failure.

____ 8. I recognize my personal management styles in handling reviews.

____ 9. I comprehend my interpersonal needs can impact a review.

____ 10. I have to accept the results and consequences of the review.

What does this assessment say? It says that a review is not only using a set of techniques such as having measurable objectives, but it includes behavioral comprehension.

FIVE-STEP REVIEW PROCESS

The review, if not handled in steps, can be most stressful for you and the person being reviewed. There can be surprises on both sides. Interpersonal relationships can be damaged permanently. The review should be against benchmarks established at the beginning of the review period by both parties. Any other issues should be handled in a separate session.

Step 1: At the beginning of the performance period (for example, the beginning of a project), together establish measurable goals.

Step 2: At project milestones, you meet to discuss performance.

Step 3: At end of the project, you should have the person do a personal evaluation.

Step 4: Do a review that includes the person's evaluation and your evaluation. Both are discussed at the same time.

Step 5: Write a final evaluation.

The measurable goals should be identified as to level of importance. The levels could be of great importance, much importance, average importance, some importance, and minimum importance. In addition, the words "all" and "100%" cannot appear. One should never give higher than "80%" as to an accepted accomplishment. Also a statement should be included that says "The objectives can be negotiated or eliminated because of the business environment."

You are courting disaster if you do not have regular meetings on performance. Silence is acceptance. It should be a scheduled time and the person should know what the subject of the meeting is. Just to call a person in for the pre-review establishes an ambiguous situation. There should be no interruptions. If possible, make sure the telephone cannot ring during the meeting. There is always the desire to react to the uninvited guest rather than the invited one.

You should have the person prepare an evaluation to bring to the review. The person should note strengths and weaknesses so you can assist where there is weakness and build on the strengths. The evaluation should be based on the accepted measurable goals, not on anything else—including other people's weaknesses and strengths.

You and the person should analyze why there are agreements and disagreements on the evaluations. The analysis should not just be on the disagreements. This is a time to look at the past so a better future can be considered.

You should write the evaluation based, when possible, on consensus. Look for ways to include the words of the person being evaluated in the final review. The review should not be a hammer of judgment, but a foundation for growth.

REVIEW SKILL SET

Based on the discussion of a review, your review skill set is straightforward:

- Be able to write measurable objectives.

- Be able to write objectives that give one the opportunity to exceed.

- Be objective.

- Preparation starts at the beginning and continues until the end of the review cycle.

WRITING A REVIEW

There are many areas where you can evaluate or review an individual. In the context of this book, the following twenty-four areas and their examples are relevant:

1. Analytical skills

    — Concentrates on analyzing essential facts such as for project X.

    — Displays strong analytical qualities such as X.

    — Handles statistical techniques to resolve problems such as X in a timely and efficient manner.

2. Communication skills (Chapters 16 and 17)

    — Asks penetrating questions in intense situations such as X.

    — Communicates with integrity and credibility in such a case as X.

    — Prevents unproductive responses in status meetings such as X.

3. Computer skills

    — Comprehends the applications so that their results exceed benchmarks and standards such as with application X.

— Demonstrates strong computer expertise especially in the area of X.

— Maximizes the benefits of computer techniques by doing X.

4. Creativity (Chapter 5)

— Challenges conventional computer practices in such areas as X.

— Demonstrates imaginative insights so that X was achieved in a timely manner.

— Explores new technical approaches and paths to achieve major breakthroughs in the area of X.

5. Decision making

— Assembles all facts prior to making a decision; in one instance, saved the company X dollars.

— Communicates decisions with confidence such as in case X.

— Makes valid decisions under pressure and has resulted in project X not failing.

6. Delegating (Chapter 7)

— Delegates while still maintaining control, which has resulted in X percentage increase in productivity.

— Matches assignments to employee skills and this has caused X.

— Recognizes the importance of working through subordinates and thus achieved X.

7. Evaluation skills (Chapter 8)

— Establishes measurable objectives so all projects were achieved on time and under budget.

— Monitors performance accurately against objectives. This has resulted in X percent productivity.

— Recognizes potentials in employees and the result has been X.

8. Innovation (Chapter 5)

— Demonstrates the skill to be innovative even under adverse conditions and this has resulted in X being accomplished.

— Develops innovative solutions that have on occasion X led to significant improvements in the network.

— Fosters an environment for innovative possibilities that has resulted in X.

9. Interpersonal skills

— Builds a climate of trust with employees, customers, and vendors so that X was achieved.

— Develops relationships based on mutual trust and on precisely defined objectives.

— Works effectively with all levels of management so that X dollars were approved for X projects.

10. Leadership (Chapter 2)

— Uses a vision to focus the group on achieving such goals as X.

— Uses leading by example to focus the group on achieving such goals as X.

— Uses training to effectively motivate the team to increase skill level such as in area X.

11. Management ability (Chapter 1)

— Applies valid management principles to achieve goals such as X.

— Develops realistic programs using measurable goals so that X was accomplished.

— Integrates objectives, skills, resources, and materials to achieve goals such as X.

12. Motivation (Chapter 4)

    — Develops optimal individual skills so the team has achieved X.

    — Looks for the best in the worst and this has resulted in X.

    — Uses positive reinforcement to motivate so the team can achieve all goals in a timely manner.

13. Negotiating skills (Chapter 11)

    — Keeps conflicts from arising such as in case X.

    — Possesses strong facilitating skills such as X that have resulted in Y.

    — Possesses strong negotiating skills such as X that have resulted in Y.

14. Oral expression (Chapter 16)

    — Develops polished and organized speeches so that X has resulted.

    — Possesses superior verbal skills so that X has been achieved.

    — Speaks effectively on feet, thus was selected to speak to customer X.

15. Organizing (Chapter 10)

    — Avoids over-staffing so there has to be a minimal requirement in the budget for positions in the group.

    — Builds on organizational effectiveness to achieve X.

    — Makes the most of the group's potential to achieve X.

16. Presentation skills (Chapter 18)

    — Develops organized and polished presentations so that upper management accepts the goals of all presentations given.

    — Prepares persuasive presentations so goals are sold to the audiences such as in case X.

    — Uses interpersonal skills to achieve the audience's respect so they agree to the stated goals.

17. Problem solving

    — Demonstrates the skill to identify, analyze, and resolve troublesome technical problems especially in the area of X.

    — Uses a practical approach in solving problems such as X.

    — Uses creativity and innovative solutions to achieve resolutions for difficult problems such as in case X.

18. Quality (Chapter 20)

    — Achieves the highest standard of excellence so that X has happened.

    — Emphasizes total quality control and assurance so that product had no errors.

    — Uses technical benchmarks and standards of excellence to achieve goal X.

19. Selling skills (Chapter 13)

    — Demonstrates the skill to sell ideas so that IT goal X was funded.

    — Uses creative selling techniques in presentations so that goals are approved for the IT group such as X.

    — Uses marketing goals to define IT goals clearly so that X is achieved.

20. Supervisory skills (Chapter 2)

    — Effectively balances work flow so that X was accomplished.

    — Maximizes use of skills, resources, and materials especially in instance X.

    — Optimizes productivity so the team did more than a team twice the size.

21. Team skills (Chapter 9)

    — Implements self-directed teams so X was achieved.

    — Maximizes skills of the team so that X was accomplished.

    — Resolves team conflicts with adroitness such as in case X.

22. Technical skills

    — Makes effective and efficient use of technical support for network applications such as X.

    — Uses cutting-edge technologies to achieve goals such as X.

    — Uses knowledge of technology to reduce costs, resources, and materials.

23. Time management (Chapter 19)

    — Eliminates time wasters so that project X was achieved earlier than stated by X days.

    — Maximizes peak times to achieve X.

    — Uses time productively to achieve X.

24. Writing skills (Chapter 17)

    — Uses a vocabulary that is comprehensible to the audience so that X has been achieved.

    — Uses e-mail to communicate status of goals in an effective manner so that X number of meetings have been eliminated.

    — Writes documents that have achieved results that improved the productivity of the IT group by X percent.

FINAL THOUGHTS ON PERFORMANCE REVIEWS

The review process can take on many possibilities beyond the individual performance review discussed above. Here are some other ideas for your consideration:

- Have a team evaluate each others' performances. Do not use the names of the reviewers. You should give a summary of points to the person reviewed.

- Have a team evaluate itself as a whole.

- Look for the lows and the highs in evaluations.

- The review process is a set of interviews, evaluations, and a final decision (appraisal).

- A meaningful review process consists of performance benchmarks, measurable goals that are achievable and have priorities, and is not a one-time event.

ON THE CD-ROM

1. 08Overview.ppt—Chapter Overview

2. 08Feedback.doc—Feedback Skills Self-Assessment

3. 08Final.xls—Termination Checklist

4. 08Review.doc—Review Skills Self-Assessment

Section 3

IT Team Management

This section describes the basic principles of team management. The section also discusses four management styles: organizer, negotiator, facilitator, and salesperson. On occasion when discussing these four management styles, a manager or leader is referred to as *charismatic*. The charismatic leader is one who leads without seeming to command. This type of leader is full of the "spirit" which is actually self-assurance and self-confidence. If you are knowledgeable of the skill set required to be successful you might also acquire these two traits and be a charismatic IT manager.

In Chapter 9, you develop the skill to consider the appropriate basic skills in accomplishing team management. The chapter discusses such principles as being aware of group dynamics and recognizing your personal style of leadership.

Chapter 10 provides information on the importance of the team's organizational structure and its relationship to the corporate organization. The chapter explains how your management style can impact the team's structure that is on paper into reality.

In Chapter 11, you learn about the skills to manage the dynamics and process of negotiating. The chapter considers how effective negotiating can lead to achieving project goals in a successful and timely manner.

In Chapter 12, you develop the knowledge of the skills for facilitating a team for an IT project. The chapter considers the importance of diversity as to knowledge, experiences, and attitudes for the use of facilitating.

In Chapter 13, you develop knowledge about the skills to be a salesperson. This means how you influence others. The reality of life is that each of us has to sell our ideas. This chapter tries to show how to sell one's ideas effectively to a team, the customer, the vendors, and to one's upper management.

CHAPTER 9

Fundamental Foundation of IT Team Management

Objectives: At the end of this chapter, you will be able to:

- Answer the question "What is a team?" (say compared to a mob).
- Answer the question "What is team management?"
- Answer the question "What are group dynamics?"
- Identify 15 factors that can make a group a team.
- Appraise yourself as a team leader (strengths and weaknesses).
- Appraise the team (strengths and weaknesses).
- Identify the five-stage evolution of a group to a team.
- Identify a method for managing such emotions as insecurity, hostility, and jealousy.
- Comprehend the importance of performance to the team.

> **NOTE:**
>
> Prior to reading this chapter, you should take the Team Management Skills Self-Assessment. It is found on the CD-ROM (09TeamMgt.doc) and in Chapter 23.

WHAT IS A TEAM?

A team is two or more people working together to achieve a common goal or purpose. Most people associate the word "team" with sports. The measurable goal is to win, by whatever the definition of win is for that sport. In the business environment a team is usually brought together to achieve a goal. Unfortunately in many cases, the goal is not as well defined as in a sports environment. An IT project team is a cross-functional team (members from across a corporation's or company's divisions, departments or other business entities) where the goal is centered on information technology (new, update, or enhancement).

While a team forms a basic unit of work activity, the underlying process is usually poorly managed. This chapter looks at the basics of team dynamics and suggests ways to accelerate development. A premise of the discussion is that the dynamics of a team may have to be managed like a dysfunctional individual.

A team is not a group, a mob, a crowd, an assemble, a gang, a family, a herd, or a flock. A team is an organization that works for the common good rather than for the individual good. It should be able to manage itself in day-to-day situations.

Why should you have a cross-functional group rather than an IT-only group? A cross-functional group is particularly good at combining talents and providing innovative solutions to possibly unfamiliar problems. In a situation where there is no established method or the project significantly impacts corporate process, the wider skill and knowledge set of the group has a distinct advantage over that of the individual or a specialized group. An IT group might only resolve a goal in terms of programming practicality rather than user needs.

WHAT IS TEAM MANAGEMENT?

Team management skill requirements have been evolving from the beginning of creation according to Judeo-Christian traditions. There was one, but then there were two and thus team management skills began with the issue of how to handle the edict, "Do not eat of the fruit of the tree of knowledge." There are a number of various translations of this edict. The point is there was a measurable goal. Project success is determined by how well the team adheres to the project goals—or more strongly put, the edicts.

When people work in a team, there are two issues involved. First are the tasks and the problems that are involved in getting the job done. Unfortunately, this is the only issue that many teams consider and more importantly, this includes the project manager. The second issue in the process is the team's intraworkings itself, or its interpersonal dynamics. This process is the mechanism by which the team acts as a unit and not as a loose mob.

Without proper attention to this process the value of the group is diminished or even destroyed. With a little explicit management of the process, it can enhance the worth of the team to be many times the sum of the parts. It is an implicit synergy that makes teamwork attractive in corporate organizations despite the possible problems of cross- functional dynamics as represented by the individuals on the team.

Team management is having the interpersonal skills to mold a group of individuals into a team that works effectively, efficiently, and effortlessly toward a common measurable goal or set of goals. An IT team manager must do this in an environment where some of the individuals do not comprehend computer technology or jargon or are apathetic toward IT.

The point is that the team should be viewed as an important resource whose maintenance must be managed just like any other project resource. You as the IT project manager need to insure early in a project that this management is done by the team itself so that it forms a normal part of the team's activities. The challenge is to keep everyone on the same score or writing the same code.

A team of people working on a common project does not necessarily invoke the team process. If the team is managed in a totally autocratic (I say, you do) management style, there may be little opportunity for interaction relating to the work; if there are factions within the team, the process may never evolve. A challenge of an IT project manager is not to take the side of the IT representatives on the team. As project manager, you must be the central point of objective decision making or someone else on the team will be the informal project manager.

Team management can lead to a situation of cooperation, coordination, and commonly understood procedures and mores (corporate culture as in comparison to a social culture). If this situation is present within a group of people, then their performance is enhanced by their mutual support. The group becomes a team. Would you rather have a group of individuals that are self-opinionated, self-centered, and loudmouths? What would be the impacts on project performance and its ultimate success? On reflection, this situation seems to apply to some sports teams with big budgets and thus expensive tickets that have not been so successful.

WHAT IS GROUP DYNAMICS?

A group is two or more people gathered together for a rational purpose. When the group is irrational, it is a mob.

Dynamics are forces, the interrelationships between members of the group. For an IT project group, the dynamics are based on technical knowledge and expertise, culture, prior relationships, communication skills, attitudes, mores, and that nebulous thing called *personality.*

As an example of group dynamics in a group of say ten or more people, you have at least one mouse and one lion. The mouse is extremely quiet and the lion can be labeled simply the loudmouth.

The mouse is the quiet one in the corner who does not say much and has the eyes glued downward. This individual is probably the least utilized resource in the group. It is your responsibility initially to get that individual to speak out and to contribute. In turn, it is the group's responsibility to encourage and develop that person, to include the mouse in the discussion and actions, and to provide positive reinforcement each time that happens.

There is another mouse-type that is not a mouse. Perhaps a better label is *hawk.* The hawk sits quietly until everyone has slugged it out and then logically summarizes the conclusion. I have seen a software development director control meeting after meeting this way.

The lion or the loudmouth usually takes a position at the end of the table and is always a dominant member whose opinions form a disproportionate share of the discussion. It is initially the project manager's responsibility to ask whether the loudmouth might like to summarize briefly, and then ask for other views.

There is an effective method for handling group dynamics—use the written record. Because a decision is not recorded it becomes clouded and it has to be discussed again. This gives the lion another opportunity to roar. This can be avoided by recording on a whiteboard each decision as it is made. This has the further advantage that each decision is expressed in a clear and concise format.

Another method of controlling group dynamics is to give frequent and objective feedback. It is important to remember that all criticism must be neutral. It must focus on the task and not the personality. This type of feedback can be considered a form of coaching. It should reduce the destructive impact of criticism when things go badly.

The need to comprehend group dynamics is especially important when there is a project failure, a potential risk. The long-term success of a group depends upon how it deals with failure. Any failure should be explored by the group based on agreed benchmarks and standards. The group must acknowledge responsibility rather than individual members. The group should examine the causes and devise a mechanism which either monitors against or prevents repetition. A group that stands together during a risk succeeds. A group that looks for a scapegoat hangs separately.

One practice that may be useful is to delegate the agreed solution to the individual or to the functional group who made the original error. This allows the project team to demonstrate its continuing trust and the penitent to make amends.

One of the aspects of group dynamics is the deadlock. If there are opposing points of view held in the group then some type of action has to be taken. One technique that might be used to resolve the deadlock is having the forces take reverse roles and argue the positions. Perhaps new views will be established. In any case, establish a time limit for debate. In the end if the issue is not critical, toss a coin.

In some instances, effective communication can resolve group dynamic issues. Effective communication happens when both the speaker and the listener act responsibly. The speaker must actively seek to express the ideas in a clear and concise manner. The listener must actively seek to comprehend what has been said and to ask for clarification if unsure. Finally, both parties must be sure that the ideas have been correctly communicated, perhaps by the listener summarizing what was said in a different way.

Group dynamics is relationships. There are both individual and group support needs. What is necessary is that these needs are recognized and explicitly dealt with by the group. Time and resources must be allocated to this as a part of the project process.

FIFTEEN FACTORS THAT MAKE A GROUP A TEAM

A group becomes a team when it can focus on the project goals and manage itself on day-to-day project issues. The team is integrated. This means if a benchmark is required, the team determines it. If there is a problem, the team solves it. If a member performs badly, the team decides the type of change needed. If there is individual conflict, the team reviews it in context of the project goals. The project manager is the "captain of the ship" rather than a member of the crew.

The team comprehends the importance of clearly defined actions. In any project, the clarity of the goals is of paramount importance. The performance of work is equal to the level of the statement of work's clarity. First, suppose that there is an 80 percent chance (80–20 rule) that a team member comprehends the goal correctly. Second, if there are 12 team members then the chance all are working toward that same goal is 2.4 percent.

The first responsibility of the team is to clarify the project goals as given by the customer and to record this comprehension so that it can be constantly seen. This project statement may be revised or replaced, but it should always act as a focus for the team's deliberations and actions. If you cannot get to common ground, then you have a group not a team.

What other factors make a group a team beyond self-management and the ability to search for clarity? Here are 13 other factors:

1. Team complements the positive aspects of corporate culture.

2. Team accepts responsibility and accountability for actions as one rather than at the individual level.

3. Team shares in decisions, results, and rewards.

4. Team uses the project process to meet goals rather than challenging it at every milestone.

5. Team works with change rather than reacting to change.

6. Team appreciates how a project can impact their complete lives.

7. Team redesigns itself when necessary to ensure the project goals are met on time and within budget.

8. Team works within the parameters of the project's measurable goals.

9. Team perceives that quality performance is the basis for success.

10. Team seeks to negotiate differences between the project goals and various functional goals.

11. Team has a high level of trust.

12. Teams have shared interests that use the project goals as the foundation.

13. Team members are supportive of each other.

SELF APPRAISAL AS A TEAM MANAGER

The first question you need to ask yourself is "What is my skill set to handle the performance variables associated with a team?" The performance variables are discussed in the next section.

You have to appraise yourself not as a manager of a corporate entity, of an individual, or of a group. The appraisal fundamentally comes down to the answer to the question, "Does the team have the capability to manage itself in a day-to-day situation and is it working toward the project goals in an effective, efficient, and effortless manner?" Hello, maker of wine from water. The degree to which you can answer yes is the degree of success you can expect for the project.

> **NOTE:**
> ____
>
> See in Chapter 1 the skill profile of a tactical (project) manager.

APPRAISAL OF THE GROUP AS A TEAM

The most important performance variable of a team is its capability to manage itself on day-to day operations. This means the project manager is the interface of the team to the customer and the rest of the outside world. The project manager is actively involved in getting the resources, materials, and equipment required to support the effort to accomplish the project's measurable goals.

Beyond this variable, there are at least four broad categories or variables for determining team performance. The position here is that there is a difference between group and team performance. The four categories are:

- Leadership (operational managers, rather than the tactical [project] manager)

- Organization

- Stakeholders

- Task

Some of the variables that should be used to do an appraisal of the performance of leadership include working with project peers, making decisions, communicating appropriate project status for function, managing within the project goals, facilitating tasks, and assisting to resolve conflicts. In addition, is there a perception that the manager is creative, trustworthy, respected, knowledgeable, and credible?

When one talks about organizational variables, it is not about the chart drawn on a piece of paper, but the interpersonal dynamics or the working relationships. One looks at the availability of benchmarks and standards for determining performance, climate, authority structure beyond the one held by the project manager, and culture or corporate mores. One can make even one additional step and look at the team's mores.

Many of the people skills discussed for a project manager are also applicable to an operational manager. See in Chapter 1 the skill profile of an operational manager for a project. These skills can be put into five broad categories: communication; people involvement; technical and business knowledge; capabilities to manage risk, time, and conflict; and project commitment.

Task-related variables are based on the core principle of quality product on time and within budget. Can the manager handle innovation and change? Upper management is always searching for the manager who can perform to get the maximum output for the minimum of input.

GROUP TO TEAM EVOLUTION

One technique of team management is to work within the framework of the evolution of a group into a team. A view of this cycle is one of five stages:

- Formation
- Assertion
- Normalization
- Performance
- Integration

Formation is the initial stage when the group comes together; the first meeting. Most of the group is usually polite and very dull. There is always the instance where some of the group has worked with or against each other. Conflict is seldom voiced directly, personal or destructive. Since the group is new, the individuals are guarded in their opinions and generally reserved. This is particularly so in terms of those individuals who tend to muddle through their thoughts to get to answers, or individuals who are new to the corporate culture. The group tends to defer to those who emerge as leaders. Actually this is where the IT project manager needs to be on solid ground and use effective and efficient skills to handle the meeting. The following are 18 of the actions you should take so there is only one project manager:

1. Strategic manager should be present to state that you have sufficient authority to do the job, and that the project goals are consistent with those of the corporation.

2. At all times seek the center.

3. Have a published agenda.

4. Have a set of measurable goals from the customer.

5. Call each individual to ensure their attendance at the first meeting.

6. Start on time (some people state their position by being late).

7. Keep to the agenda.

8. Support contributions from all the members.

9. Ensure that you have verbal agreement from all the members.

10. Seek contrasting views.

11. Test for a decision.

12. Get a group decision.

13. Assign roles and responsibilities.

14. Get an agreement on accountability of actions and dates.

15. Establish the next step of the whole team.

16. Establish the time and place of the next meeting.

17. End on time.

18. Write the minutes of the meeting.

Assertion is the next stage. This stage can be minimized by doing all the steps above except the first one. This is the stage where there is dissension. Some of the possible events are factions forming, personalities clashing, no one conceding a single point without a fight first. It is important as the IT project manager not to permit even the beginning of the IT versus non-IT factions. In addition, very little constructive communication occurs. If it is bad, you have a set of monologues with no dialog. You need to watch for sarcasm, invectiveness, and imputation. To get to the assertion stage you need to do private negotiations to clarify positions and write the meeting minutes eliminating strident terminology. Instead of saying "John demanded so-and-so," say, "John's position is so-and-so."

The next stage is the normalization. This is to get everyone to focus on accomplishing the measurable project goals. The emphasis is on *measurable* because you have an objective foundation as a work platform. Get away from the person and to the business. At this stage, the factions may recognize the merits of working together and the in-fighting subsides. You should also expect a new spirit of cooperation to be present, as every group member begins to feel secure in expressing their own viewpoints and these are discussed openly with the whole group. The most important situation is that people start listening to each other. Work methods become the priority, or more appropriately, the project process becomes the foundation of discussions rather than personal positions.

The fourth stage is the impact of performance. As a part of the project process, you should have some milestones that are achievable early so you can point to project steps that have been achieved. Nothing is better to develop trust than success. This stage is the beginning of when the group has settled on a system which allows free and frank exchange of views. In addition, there should be support by the group for each other.

Integration is the final stage. A team ceases to be a group when it works for the common good rather than the individual good. In addition, it manages itself in day-to-day situations.

MANAGEMENT OF THE IRRATIONAL

There are many schools of personal behavior on how to manage such emotions as insecurity, hostility, and jealousy. However, this discussion is on using the concept of Return on Investment (ROI) as the basis of any team management issue. Rather than handling emotions behaviorally using cultural mores or psychology (you really were not trained to be a psychologist), you work in terms of business values. One person might think the person's data are too valuable to share with anyone else. You have to argue how sharing the data improves the value of the data to the project and to the corporation.

Return on Investment (ROI) is usually thought of in direct financial benefits. However, there are many indirect benefits, which might be considered ROI and can be used by you to manage and control the project management process as it relates to team management. The list below shows broad areas where you might find benefits generated by a project. Below are six broad areas with some sub-divisions that you can use as starting points in discussions to resolve emotional issues that raise their ugly heads through the team.

- Common environment
  - Core training environment
  - Common tools
  - Streamlined processes
- Decentralized working environment (offices)
- Enhanced productivity

- Information efficiencies
    - Easier and faster access
    - Increase in accuracy and availability
    - Increase in communication, resources, and timeliness
    - More marketing data
    - More technical sources
- Opportunities for
    - New roles
    - New skills or enhancements
- Reductions in
    - Documentation costs
    - Duplicative resources
    - Ordering time
    - Search effort time
    - Support costs

IMPORTANCE OF TEAM PERFORMANCE

Earlier in the chapter, four broad categories or variables for determining team performance were discussed. The position here is there is a difference between group and team performance. The four categories are:

- Leadership (operational managers, rather than the tactical [project] manager)
- Organization
- Stakeholders
- Task

Beyond the variables, you have to consider performance ends that are fundamentally emotional. These emotional goals are as powerful as any of the personal emotions such as anger and jealousy. When you handle project management you must consider these performance ends during the project and not in a casual manner after project completion. One does not simply say "Oh by the way that was a good job." The four performance ends are as follows:

- Achievement

- Advancement

- Recognition

- Responsibility

Prior to having the first project meeting, your duty is to work with the strategic manager and the customer to develop a set of achievable goals. During the initial planning meeting, you need to get group agreement or alternatives to the goals that based on known knowledge are achievable. If the goals are unrealistic, the team has a sense of failure immediately. If the goals are too easy, the team feels little. There should be a series of milestones, which are easily recognized as stages toward the ultimate completion of the goals. Thus progress is punctuated and celebrated with incremental marked achievements. The team needs to see the light at the end of the tunnel. Rather than having one long, long tunnel, you need many short tunnels.

There are two types of advancement: the long-term issues such as promotion, salary raises, and job prospects that you do not necessarily control; and the short-term issues that you control that include increased responsibility, the acquisition of new skills, and broader experience. Your team members are looking for the former. You have to provide the latter and convince them that these are necessary to achieve the former. The project environment cannot be a situation where a member senses that when the project is done, everything goes back as it was prior to the project. One has to be careful of project titles because project members may desire to keep the title in their business environments.

Recognition is being appreciated. It is to know that what you do is seen and noted. Recognition should not only come from you, but also from the team, the strategic manager, and the member's personal manager. The attitude that "no one cares" is deadly to the present project, and even more so to the next project. Recognition should be an ongoing action during the project. It should not be a form letter six months after the completion of the project. Worse is no letter at all!

The feedback (recognition) you give your team about their work is fundamental to their motivation. Each should know what is being done well (positive), what needs improving (constructive), and what is expected (achievable).

A sense of responsibility is the most lasting of these four performance ends. When one gains responsibility it is seen as an advancement, which gives rise to a sense of achievement and can improve the performance. Giving responsibility is a part of the skill of delegating authority. Also there are two components of responsibility, individual and team.

ON THE CD-ROM

1. 09Overview.ppt—Chapter Overview

2. 09TeamMgt.doc—Team Management Skills Self-Assessment

3. 09TeamAsmt.xls—Team Assessment

CHAPTER 10

The Organizer:
Placement of the Players

Objectives: At the end of this chapter, you will be able to:

- Answer the question "What is an organization?"

- Identify skills to be an organizer.

- Answer the question, "What does it mean to organize?"

- Answer the question, "What are the dynamics of an organization?"

- Identify three types of team organizations.

- Contrast the paper organization versus the actual organization.

- Identify eight challenges to the organization because of decentralization.

This chapter provides you with information on the importance of the IT organizational structure and its relationship to the corporate organization. This chapter explains how your management style can impact the structure that is on paper in actuality.

NOTE:

Prior to reading this chapter, you should take the Organizing Skills Self-Assessment. It is found on the CD-ROM (10Organ.doc) and in Chapter 23.

WHAT IS AN ORGANIZATION?

An organization is two or more people gathered together for a common goal and the goal cannot be achieved by an individual or only by some of the people. It is an ordered whole. The goal may be for just a game of gin. While the two players are together to play, the environment is ordered. It has elements to achieve a set of functions.

An IT organization is a group, unit, or team. It has the function of handling the operations and services involved with the maintenance and update of a computerized environment with the prime purpose of transmitting data from one point to another. This organization has its own unique technical jargon. In fact, any organization has its own unique jargon to identify its members. The IT organization has clients and servers, while training has students and classrooms.

A recent organizational theory holds that an organization is a living organism. From this it can be implied that an organizer's skill set includes knowledge of types of:

- Environments
  - Local
  - National
  - International
  - Business
  - Government
  - Industry
  - Technical
- Inputs
  - Skills
  - Materials
  - Money
  - Information

- Outputs
  - Products
  - Services
  - Waste
  - Satisfaction
- Transformers
  - Managerial
  - Technical
  - Human
  - Support (training and documentation)
  - Corporate culture

SKILLS TO BE AN ORGANIZER

What makes the skills of an organizer different from any other skill set? The basic difference is structure. Other related words to structure are configuration, system, group, order, unit, and team. An organizer is concerned with process. An organizer can be simply the one who asks another to play gin. One corporation had a group president who went to an established organization to reorganize them, or he started a new organization by being its first member. The latter part of his career he was an "organizer."

The organizer can be identified sometimes by the questions asked:

- What is the goal or purpose of the organization?
- What are the boundaries of the organization?
- What is the state of the organization?
- Should the organization exist?
- Are the functions appropriate for the organization?

NOTE:

While the word organization is used in the five questions, an organizer might use any of these words: division, group, unit, or team.

Some people think of an organizer as a leader. While leadership has been a systematic study for seventy plus years, the professionals of this area would not accept this as an absolute comparison. Skills of an organizer would include the following:

- Direct a group toward a common goal.

- Use the communication process to gain interpersonal influence.

- Rationally go beyond the corporate routine directives to gain influence.

- Convince others to do something while making it appear as an art.

- Interpret events for followers.

- Actions are observable and others try to imitate them.

- Establish objectives for others.

- Maintain cooperative relationships.

- Subscribe to the idea of commonality.

- Commonly use a phrase such as "The team did this."

The "doing" is important to being a successful organizer. However, the underpinnings of the skills are a set of traits. Remember a trait is unobservable and may not have measurable results. Some of the traits of a successful organizer include:

- Achievement oriented

- Honest

- Has integrity
- Knowledgeable of the business
- Perceptive
- Self-confident
- Self-motivated
- Tenacious

WHAT DOES IT MEAN TO ORGANIZE?

The organizer uses the organization to:

- Challenge the status quo.
- Communicate direction.
- Develop strategies based on a vision.
- Motivate itself.
- Set a direction.

Within a corporation, a common label for an organizer is *builder.* An organizer uses the standard functions of management—planning, developing, designing, staffing, budgeting, and controlling—in the context of an organization. The individual does not negotiate; the organization negotiates. The organization is the organizer in reality.

To use the skills of an organizer one first must be knowledgeable about the dynamics of an organization. Second, the organizer must comprehend the importance of the various types of organization. As with any skill set, skills used are based on some related knowledge base.

An organizer can be labeled a "boss," "tyrant," "negotiator," or one of many labels. The emphasis is on managing the dynamics of an organization.

Like any other manager, the organizer has an underpinning of behaviors based on attitudes, assumptions, knowledge, and existing skill sets.

Based on what has been stated up to this point about an organizer, perhaps a more formal definition of the management skill set can be presented. An organizer is a manager who seeks to integrate the formal and human (informal) organizations, the associated internal and external environments, inputs, outputs, and transformers as one framework.

WHAT ARE THE DYNAMICS OF AN ORGANIZATION?

A *dynamic* as used here means the interplay among individuals to achieve a goal. Each person may have a distinct perception of the goal. A basic skill of an organizer is to organize the group so all have the same goal perception.

The fundamental dynamic in any organization is how it perceives itself. Other organization dynamics are based on how the group seeks to:

- Accept responsibility and accountability for actions.

- Appreciate how a project can impact their complete lives.

- Complement the positive aspects of corporate culture.

- Develop a high level of trust.

- Perceive that quality performance is the basis for success.

- Redesign itself when necessary to ensure the group goals are met.

- Seek to negotiate differences between the group goals and various functional goals.

- Share in decisions, results, and rewards.

- Use a process to meet goals rather than challenging it at every milestone.

- Work with change rather than reacting to change.

- Work within the parameters of measurable goals.

- Share interests that use the group's goals as the foundation.

- Support each other.

IDENTIFY STRUCTURE TYPES OF ORGANIZATIONS

The traditional organization's structure is of course the "tree" type. There is one individual, then a second level of managers, and more levels as thought necessary. In a large corporation, this tree is not as straightforward as one thinks. A manager can actually be higher on the tree than a vice president, but without the pay or perceived authority (personal experience). As corporations seek to be involved in international markets, new types of organizations are being developed. However, for the purposes of this book we will only look at some of the organizational structures of a project team. Why look at project teams? An IT organization, probably more than any other group, as a whole has to be organized into project teams. Sometimes these teams are formalized with the corporate structure, but in more cases they are not because of day-to-day operational requirements. The three structures for teams that are discussed below are coordinated, hierarchical, and interconnected.

Coordinated Structure

The first model puts the program manager as the centerpiece or hub of the team. The handicap of this model is the project manager can easily lose control because in reality decisions are reached by the team members on the circle's rim. The project manager may or may not learn about critical decisions. The project manager may manage, but not control. Figure 10-1 is an example of a coordinated project team structure.

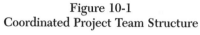

Figure 10-1
Coordinated Project Team Structure

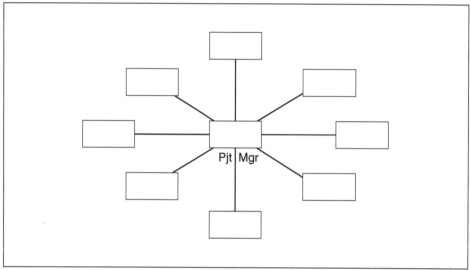

Hierarchical Structure

The second model puts the program manager as the top of the team. The handicap of this model is that the project manager is the decision maker and the source of all information. This makes the decision-making process one that is declarative rather than one based on negotiation. Figure 10-2 is an example of a hierarchical project team structure.

Figure 10-2
Hierarchical Project Team Structure

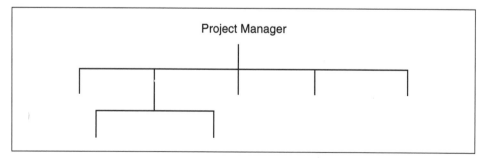

Interconnected Structure

The third model puts the program manager as the top of the team; however, there are connections among all the team members. There now is a place for decision making to be a negotiating process, but the project manager still represents a source of authority. Figure 10-3 is an example of an interconnected project team structure.

Figure 10-3
Interconnected Project Team Structure

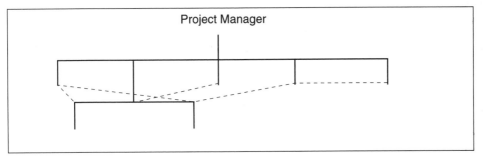

PAPER ORGANIZATION VERSUS THE ACTUAL ORGANIZATION

As an IT group manager you may have a formal corporate organization chart to account for heads. However, you as an organizer could use any of the three project team structures if you are aware of them and you use the interpersonal dynamics caused by these three structures. No matter how large your IT organization, the interconnected structure can produce positive results. Why does this model have a high potential for success? Your staff accepts that they do not work in isolation from each other. Even if the corporate structure is reorganized, the staff has a habit of working with each other. The importance of function becomes second to interpersonal relationships. You might be surprised at the informal interconnections that already exist in your IT organization.

What causes an organization to be different from the one on paper? Besides the interpersonal dynamics there are a number of forces that also play their part, including:

- Corporate values and culture

- Size

- Number of functions

- Experience-level mix

- Internal and external perceptions of the IT group

Assess for yourself the type of IT organization based on whether your corporation is technologically oriented or has some other focus. Are the corporate values helpful to the growth of the IT organization? What are the values that hinder?

Size can affect an organization as to everyone knowing everyone else. When you get beyond 500 your group probably loses a sense of "village." The larger the group, the more defined are the processes and the loss of flexibility.

When you have a basic function such as writing code to make a product work, you have a very tight sense of community that can use all available resources, materials, and equipment. What happens when you have three product lines? There is competition for resources, materials, equipment, and most importantly, skills.

When the organization is small, your experienced employees may just ignore the inexperienced ones. The more skilled staff may simply desire to get the job done. You have to manage an "it is quicker to do it myself" attitude. As the organization grows each team leader wants the most skilled staff because training and development takes time. Actually the first scenario and second may be the same. You just have to manage groups rather than individuals.

Perceptions of any shade can have an impact on an organization. A perception of potential success can develop into achievements better than negative expectations. Perception is a basis for customer satisfaction.

DECENTRALIZATION CHALLENGES TO THE ORGANIZATION

The trend of decentralization in large corporations can certainly have an impact on the management of an IT organization. Here are eight potential issues of decentralization:

- Personal management skills have to be enhanced over technical skills.

- Teleconferencing skills have to be developed.

- The "hallway" environment has to be created to overcome personal isolation.

- Measured goals and defined completion dates or milestones have to be a requirement.

- Conflict management will have new opportunities because of increased misunderstandings created by personal isolationism.

- All members take an equal degree of importance to support the personal isolationism.

- Oral and written communication skills will take on a new importance because of limited face-to-face encounters.

- Empowerment and trust will take on new meanings.

ON THE CD-ROM

1. 10Overview.ppt—Chapter Overview
2. 10Organ.doc—Organizing Skills Self-Assessment

CHAPTER 11

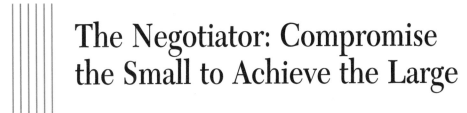

The Negotiator: Compromise the Small to Achieve the Large

Objectives: At the end of this chapter, you will be able to:

- Answer the question, "What are negotiations?"
- Identify the differences between individual and group negotiations.
- State the steps for preparing to negotiate.
- Answer the question, "What are the dynamics of negotiating?"
- Identify two techniques for negotiating.
- Identify skills to become a negotiator.
- Identify eight tactics possible during a win-lose situation.

In this chapter, you learn about the skills to manage the dynamics and process of negotiating. The chapter considers how effective negotiating can lead to achieving project goals in a successful and timely manner.

Everyone negotiates. Many people are unaware that they are negotiating and often end up with the worst part of a deal. You can especially lose when you are negotiating with someone who is aware of the concepts and techniques necessary for effective negotiation. You should never rely purely on your instinctive skills to get through a negotiation. You should use a skill set that results in a win-win negotiation.

NOTE:

Prior to reading this chapter, you should take the Negotiating Skills Self-Assessment. It is in Chapter 23 and on the CD-ROM (11Negotiate.doc).

What are Negotiations?

A negotiation in its simplest form occurs when two or more people are gathered together to reach an agreement or to decide the terms for an agreement. A common business result is a contract. An agreement does not mean a compromise; it means accepted results by the parties. One of the parties may be very unhappy, as were the Germans after the negotiations that ended World War I. As an IT manager what can you learn from this historical event? The answer is simple; when you negotiate, try to ensure that none of the parties are too unhappy.

The basic skill sets of negotiations are oral and written communication. Perhaps a successful negotiator is also a successful salesperson.

Negotiation is part of life, business and every day. As you take on more responsibility, the complexity of the negotiations increases. As your responsibility increases so does the need for negotiating experience. Is this statement valid? You probably have found yourself negotiating high-level deals with relatively inexperienced but highly motivated people. These people perceive negotiation as a game of winners and losers. In these situations, conflict and deadlocks are commonplace. Diversities in culture and language only escalate negotiating issues.

Negotiations can be put into three categories. The first two are for game players, not negotiators. The three categories are:

1. I lose; you win.
2. I win; you lose.
3. We both win.

In reality, the first two categories are both lose-lose situations. Just remember the Germans after they signed the peace treaty. You cannot have an IT contract (project plan) where the customer or you feel like you are on the losing side of the agreement.

INDIVIDUAL AND GROUP NEGOTIATIONS

Individual negotiations are a process of one-on-one. Examples of this type of negotiations are the hiring process and the review process. Group negotiations are the ones that affect more than two individual negotiators. The major example for an IT group is any project plan where the IT staff plays a significant role in the results or consequences of achieving the project's goals.

One of the impacts of getting to group negotiations is the level of managerial decision making. Five steps lead from individual decision making to group negotiations based on the manager's position. The five steps are as follows:

- The manager makes a decision without consulting anyone (not really negotiations by definition).

- The manager asks for information from others, then makes a decision (same as the first, but others involved).

- The manager consults for information from individuals, then makes a decision (same as the second, except there is now interaction).

- The manager consults for information from the group, then makes a decision (same as the second, except there is now interaction).

- The manager explains the issues to the group and the group negotiates the decision.

A number of factors go into achieving a successful negotiation. One could say attitude, attitude, and attitude; but in reality, there are other factors. However, if the attitude of the parties is not "we both win," the following six factors are not important:

- Quality technical decision
- Structured problem
- Negotiations reflect organizational goals
- Sufficient information
- Commitment by negotiators
- Acceptability to parties involved, but not directly involved in the negotiations

PREPARING TO NEGOTIATE

Before you walk into a room, you have to do five prior activities beyond developing within yourself the attitude that we both can mutually win. The five activities are:

- Define one's requirements, needs, or desires.
- Define the issues.
- Determine what can be traded.
- Establish an offense and defense.
- Hold with one's principles.

WHAT ARE THE DYNAMICS OF NEGOTIATING?

As has been discussed earlier in the chapter, there are three broad perceptions of what negotiations are. The first two are based on games, while the third is based on adult interpersonal relationships. The three categories are Win-Lose, Lose-Win, and Win-Win situations.

However, within these three categories you have to consider the dynamics of negotiating caused by:

- The negotiators' personalities

- The negotiators' skills and abilities

- The organizational climate

- The negotiating staffs' personalities

- The size of the negotiating team

- The perceptions of external staff (management and employees)

These dynamics are discussed further in the chapter's section on a negotiator's skill set. However, one example may demonstrate these dynamics. What if you are working with a customer and the customer comes from an organization that is highly competitive and holds as a part of its culture that it must win?

TECHNIQUES FOR NEGOTIATING

There are at least two techniques for enhancing negotiations. They can be used except in a highly formal and structured negotiating environment. The two techniques are brainstorming and nominal group technique.

Brainstorming plays to the irrational; that is, innovative and creative problem solving. The ground rules are as follows:

- Spontaneity is permitted no matter how extreme.

- Ideas belong to the group.

- Ideas can be reworked as frequently as required.

- All ideas are on the table before there is any analysis.

The nominal group technique plays to the rational; that is, there is a focus on a structured problem-solving process. The ground rules are as follows:

- Ideas are written down first.

- There is a sharing of ideas one at a time and this continues until all individuals have shared their ideas.

- Discussion is based on clarification not criticism.

- Voting is done to reduce alternatives.

- There is in-depth discussion of the surviving alternatives.

- Voting is done to find the most acceptable solution.

SKILLS TO BE A NEGOTIATOR

The skill set of a negotiator should be based on the awareness required to manage the dynamics of a negotiation. The first thing is to become aware of the attitudes of negotiators as to the win-win situation.

A part of your skill set is to know how your personality might affect the decision-making process. Are you flexible in coming to a solution? Is it important to you that others be involved in decision making? What is being said here is that you usually take the baggage of your day-to-day operational decision-making position into the negotiating conference room.

The next part of the negotiator's skill set is the ability to do problem solving. The big item here of course is conflict management or resolution. A goal of negotiating is to have a structured problem. The problem should be one where all have a common comprehension of its definition.

A fourth component is to be aware of the organizational dynamics involved in the negotiations. The dynamics are in two parts, internal and external. The internal dynamics may appear to be running smoothly one day and roughly the next. Why is there this change in dynamics? Perhaps the other negotiator reported results back to the external organization and it has a "we must win all the cookies" attitude.

A fifth component is to assign responsibilities and authority if the negotiating is large, such as the development of a complex IT project. You need to define one very important negotiating boundary within which everyone works, that is, a structured problem. You would not negotiate as a structured problem "the customer needs a server."

A sixth component is determining the resources required to achieve successful results. This could be included in the list of preparing for negotiations; however, it includes the resources that are determined *from* the negotiations.

After identifying these six components, what are you really trying to do as a negotiator? Perhaps an answer is that you are trying to develop a process of consensus. This process is arriving at a decision that all members will support. The resolution may be acceptable, although not necessarily the most agreeable one. Why should you want to achieve a consensus? A consensus may result in creativity and innovation.

TACTICS OF A WIN-LOSE NEGOTIATION

While your goal is to achieve a win-win situation, the other negotiator may not have the same goal. Eight possible tactics that might be used by a negotiator in a win-lose situation are the following:

- Pushing the envelope, that is, testing your boundaries

- Being emotional by stating such things as "you are being unfair" in your terms

- Making threats by stating there will be penalties if you do not agree

- Making ambiguous statements that seem to state more than is

- Insulting your company's capabilities or even your competence

- Intimidating you through such actions as keeping you waiting or leaving the room during negotiations

- Asking leading questions that have the purpose of getting you to state a weakness

- Dividing and conquering—probably the most nasty of these tactics because there is an attempt to play your team members against each other

Your positions should be as follows:

- Stay firm to your defined measurable goals.

- You need to restate your position for a balanced settlement when called "unfair."

- When a threat is made, you have to state that negotiations cannot continue until there has been a review of the matter.

- When an ambiguous statement is made, you need to ask for clarification before negotiations can continue.

- Stay calm by remembering it is not personal, only business.

- Always bring other work so when you are kept waiting you can be productive.

- You need to avoid answering leading questions.

- The team should be briefed as to your expectations and any concerns should be discussed with you outside of the negotiating room during an adjournment.

ON THE CD-ROM

1. 11Overview.ppt—Chapter Overview
2. 11Negotiate.doc—Negotiating Skills Self-Assessment

CHAPTER 12

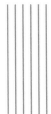

The Facilitator:
Balance of the Push and Pull
of the Project Process

Objectives: At the end of this chapter, you will be able to:

- Answer the question "What is facilitating?"
- Identify ten skills of a facilitator.
- Answer the question, "Is facilitating more than touching and feeling?"
- Define an environment for facilitating.
- Identify six categories that act as potential blocks to facilitating.

In this chapter, you develop the knowledge of the skills for facilitating a team for an IT project. The chapter considers the importance of diversity as to knowledge, experiences, and attitudes for the use of facilitating.

NOTE:

Before reading this chapter, you should take the Facilitating Skills Self-Assessment found on the CD-ROM (12Facil.doc). It is also found in Chapter 23.

WHAT IS FACILITATING?

To be a facilitator means to have the skills to be successful with diverse teams and groups inside and outside your IT organization.

Team or *group* as used in this chapter means "small." As you get closer to thirty, or even two dozen, the less group cohesion can be expected. There is a tendency to lose some of the group. A hockey team has only twenty active players and goalies at any time, thus the coach could be considered a facilitator. I am sure that this number was not established to acknowledge the theory of facilitating, but this number has been determined through experience to be effective and efficient for team management. We sometimes come in the back door to achieve some sets of skills.

Notice the word "individual" has not been used. When considering the skill set of a facilitator on a one-to-one basis, consider them relevant to the skill set of a mentor or personal coach.

SKILLS OF A FACILITATOR

The word *facilitate* comes from Italian meaning, "transport the students." In standard English, to facilitate means "to make easier." So one can say a facilitator makes things easier. What does that mean as to skills? Ten skills that relate to being a facilitator are as follows:

1. Respect others.

2. Accept individual differences.

3. Allow for another individual's uniqueness.

4. Be supportive.

5. Use two-way communication.

6. Listen to others' views with openness.

7. Recognize the potential conflict for differences.

8. Use feedback.

9. Do not be overly concerned about disagreement.

10. Accept ambiguity.

Is Facilitating More Than Touching and Feeling?

Some people tend to relate facilitating with "touch-and-feel"; however, it is more than that. First, there is an acknowledgment that a skill set can be based on behavioral factors. Second, there must be ways to measure a facilitator's skill set. For example, you can demonstrate how you respect others. Do you permit others to express their ideas and then state that another person's idea is equal or better than the idea you have given? This is a goal of facilitating; that within a group the "mouse" and "lion" personality types are both heard. These two personality types are discussed more in Chapter 9.

Creating an Environment for Facilitating

Facilitating is one of a number of specialized skill sets used to manage group dynamics. It is a skill set for small groups rather than for large groups and individuals. As in all forms of management, there is a label for the knowledge of working with a small group and the label is *emergent social system.* The theory is that a small group, even one organized in a classroom environment, will perform a task based on predictable patterns. If something is true for a classroom, then could it be true for a day-to-day operational environment? The answer is not necessarily correct. Note the word "correct" is used instead of "true." You can measure the degree of correctness, but not truthfulness. The problem is the external and internal forces that do not exist in the classroom, such as telephone calls and interpersonal relationships.

A goal of facilitating is to establish a process in a classroom environment that can become a set of positive habits in the work environment. One of the important functions of facilitating is making people aware of corporate diversity that includes gender, race, and culture. Some people are not conscious that telling a joke that relates to diversity may seriously offend someone else in the group. This idea applies equally to prohibiting center-folds from either *Playboy* or *Playgirl* on a staff's wall.

Facilitating is the skill set that focuses on the feelings of the group rather than your personal feelings. However, your personal feelings are important to the mix. The way you treat others may spill over to how others in the group treat each other.

How is this discussion important to an IT manager? You have a unique type of diversity, programmers and nonprogrammers. If you treat one group differently from the other group, what does this say to the whole group? What happens if the programmers as a group think of themselves as "better" or more important than the rest of the group? What happens when you have a superstar who forgets that without the group there would be no superstar? These issues might be resolved on an individual basis, but doubtful. In a group situation where everyone is treated on an equal basis, perhaps more of the group will become aware of interpersonal relationships that can be improved day-to-day.

POTENTIAL BLOCKS TO FACILITATING

You need to be aware of the potential operational blocks beyond those related to the classroom blocks such as group size. The operational blocks are the ones that are developed in the facilitating classroom environment. The six broad categories are:

- Composition and diversity level
- Leadership styles
- Processes
- Purpose
- Structure
- Working environment

Composition and diversity level of a group or the corporation have been discussed earlier. What are the specific factors that can impact facilitating? There are three broad categories that are related to each group member: attributes, demographic characteristics, and needs. Attributes include qualifications (knowledge and skills), personality, and value structure. Demographic characteristics include the big three: age, gender, and race. Individual needs include job security, job growth, and job recognition. One of the questions that can be raised is "What are the differences between a group with an average age of twenty-seven and a group that is forty-seven?"

You might ask, "How can a group's purpose be a blocker to facilitating?" How specified is your group's purpose? Out of purpose come tasks and requirements; these are two of the foundations for many project issues. The issues lead to the need for conflict management. When this happens, you know that the facilitating process has broken down.

Leadership styles here are not to be equated with management styles. What leadership style means is the technique used by individuals in the informal structure to pull and push other individuals toward a given goal. The danger is that the goal may not be the one necessary for the group as a whole to succeed. Two leadership styles can be identified as *interpreters* and *actors*. The first defines performance, while the second creates performance. The issue here is a type of activity that can create subgroups very quickly and cause the whole project to go up in smoke or in flames.

Both informal and formal processes can impact facilitating. These processes impact group development and performance. Perhaps a lack of a process should also be included. What if you do not have a structured project process and your group must get a product out to market with a tight deadline and under budget? The potential stress can break down any results from a facilitating activity. It might be important to bring the group together for a day to look at where the group stands on matters that might be facilitated. The area that studies the impacts of processes is called *boundary management.*

Structure is concerned with roles, size, subgroups, technological awareness, and values. Within a group, there are roles—and the larger the group, the more role differentiation you have. Some of the roles are formal such as manager or team leader. However, in many instances the informal roles are more important. The movement of ideas within a group can be enhanced by effective information seekers and givers. Do not forget the "mouse" and the "lion" in meetings. (See Chapter 9 for more on these two roles.) The larger a group the quicker the facilitating process breaks down. The larger a group the quicker it is for subgroups to form that become competitive with each other. You may think because you manage an IT group everyone has technological awareness. There may be an element of truth in this statement; however, the technological awareness may have a very narrow bandwidth. External cultural values can have an unknown impact on the group because this area is so broad. However, you need to consider the corporate values that are based on the corporate mission statement and the corporate myths. (We started with only two people in a garage.)

The working environment as defined here is both operational and corporate. One cannot ignore that one's departmental island exists within a large corporate ocean and requires the other islands in order to exist. You may have the informational database, but they have the financial and human supports for long-term existence. Besides the external environment that supports the corporate environment, we have organizational characteristics and culture that can be facilitating blocks. The organizational characteristics include your organizational structure, your technology level (use and awareness), corporate strategy, decision-making processes, working conditions that include rewards and punishments, and of course management styles and skill levels. The organizational culture includes the staff's attitudes toward the organizational characteristics, the formal and informal power structures, and corporate values.

ON THE CD-ROM

1. 12Overview.ppt—Chapter Overview
2. 12Facil.doc—Facilitating Skills Self-Assessment

CHAPTER 13

The Salesperson: Sell the Ideas

Objectives: At the end of this chapter, you will be able to:

- Answer the question, "What does it mean to be a salesperson?"
- Answer the question, "Why is selling a part of your everyday experience?"
- Identify the complexity of selling your ideas.
- Identify core components for assessing yourself as a salesperson.
- Develop a selling strategy.
- Prepare the sale of an idea.
- Use effective and efficient communication for selling.
- Comprehend how Return on Investment (ROI) can be used for selling.
- Use ROI to manage resistance to technological ideas.

You are saying, "I am an IT manager, I never sell anything. There is no good reason for me to read this chapter." You are of course incorrect. In this chapter, you develop knowledge about the skills to be a salesperson. This means how you influence others.

NOTE:

There is a Selling Skills Self-Assessment. It is found in Chapter 23 and on the CD-ROM as 13Selling.doc.

WHAT DOES IT MEAN TO BE A SALESPERSON?

The reality of life is that each of us has to sell our ideas. Selling happens any time that you meet with your staff, the customer, the vendors, or your senior management to put forward an idea that you want to be reality.

The skill set for being a successful salesperson of ideas includes using group dynamics, the perception of you by others, effective and efficient communication (oral, written, and presentation), motivation, and team management. Perhaps most important, you have to change others' perceptions into your reality.

As a salesperson, you need to comprehend 16 forces:

1. Your influence in your group and the organization

2. Your internal drivers

3. Your perception of yourself, then the real you

4. Your place in the organization

5. Your IT people skills

6. IT people skills of your staff

7. Others' drivers

8. Others' motivations

9. Others' perceptions of you

10. The crucial first impression of thirty seconds

11. The dynamic nature of an organization

12. The importance of, "as you move, so will you be seen"

13. The importance of effective and efficient communication

14. The importance of effective personal contact

15. The importance of sounding confident

16. The power and influence in relationships

Selling is a complex set of skills that is based on science and on art. You have to do research on the needs of the customer and then you have to comprehend the customer's behavior to establish a solution that is both rational and emotional.

WHY IS SELLING A PART OF MY EVERYDAY LIFE?

Your opinion as a technical person is that to be a salesperson you have to sell a product, a widget. Your network is a widget to others. It is a widget, not usually seen except as to what happens on their terminals (usually referred to as "my computer" as long as it works, "your computer" when it does not work) as far as your customers are concerned. You have to sell any changes to "my computer."

When you suggest a network change in a conversation or a presentation, you may not hear the phrase "sell me," but it is there. You might hear "convince me" or "give me the reasons for doing this change." Either phrase translates to "sell me." It comes down to marketing, trading, and dealing.

ACHIEVING YOUR GOALS THROUGH SELLING

Before you go forth to sell an idea, you must have done a core assessment. Four components of this assessment are:

- Identify where you are now and where you want to be.

- Recognize your values, that is, what it is you want in life and career.

- Determine how to make an idea happen and build your support systems.

- Identify methods for overcoming obstacles and reaching your goals.

DEVELOPING A SALES STRATEGY FOR IT

There are five basic steps in developing any sales strategy. The steps are as follows:

- Research your customer's requirements.

- Prepare a presentation based on the customer's requirements.

- Use the presentation to show that you comprehend the customer's requirements and have a solution.

- Negotiate a "win-win" sale.

- Close the sale by assuring the customer of your promises that you will keep.

Now, how are these steps applicable to you selling an idea to enhance your network? As an IT manager you probably have more data on the customer's relationship with your group than any other group has in comparison. You collect data on the network and you need to analyze this usage to see where you need to direct your attention.

Prepare a presentation that will be comprehended by the customer. Do not wrap the presentation in IS technical jargon. There will be no sale if the customer has to try to translate what you said into their jargon. The customer will continue to be unsatisfied or find an alternative solution. You are trying to sell a perception of comprehension of a need more than a widget.

You must sell based on a "win-win" solution or both parties will lose. In a "win-lose" situation, the result is an unhappy customer. In a "lose-win" situation, the result may be some risk to the network.

PREPARING TO MAKE THE SALE

There may be a number of sales techniques for preparing a sale, but it may come to a set of skills that are based on knowing:

- Know yourself.

- Know your strengths.

- Know your product.

- Know your market.

- Know your sales strategy.

- Know your customer.

- Know that selling is a step-by-step process.

- Know that selling requires attention, appetite, and action.

- Know that selling requires interest, integrity, and investment.

- Know that selling requires commitment, conviction, and communication.

SELLING THROUGH EFFECTIVE AND EFFICIENT COMMUNICATION

Chapters 16 through 18 discuss the oral, written, and presentation skills. However, when it comes to selling there are certain principles you need to follow, including the following:

- Be assertive, not aggressive.
- Be aware of your conflict management style.
- Be calm in handling awkward situations.
- Be flexible in your style of communication.
- Be positive.
- Make sure you are noticed.
- Recognize emotional triggers (yours and others').
- See the world as the other person sees it.
- Use tact in handling difficult people.
- Use three forms of communication: facts, emotions, and values.

The above principles can be summed up as, know what your customer really wants as soon as possible and be prepared to make the sale. In all cases, it has to be a "win-win" situation.

There are several writing techniques that you should use to make you better at selling. Ten of these techniques are as follows:

- Write as though the customer is present.
- Use the active voice.
- Do not use IT jargon.
- Write as you talk.
- Use a logical flow.
- Have a strong opening.
- Use short words and sentences.
- Write clearly.
- Write in a positive manner.
- Revise only when you complete the document.

Managing Resistance to Your Ideas

Many different skill sets can be used for managing resistance, but all are based on tact, integrity, and patience. The example here is based on Return on Investment (ROI). The skill is to demonstrate value for the person when support is given to an idea. A common form of resistance is the one toward technological advancement.

Return on Investment (ROI) is usually thought of in direct financial benefits. However, there are many indirect benefits which might be considered ROI. One is to sell an idea. The list below shows broad areas where you might find benefits generated from a project. Below are six areas with some sub-divisions that you can use as starting points in discussions to resolve a resistant issue.

1. Common environment
    — Applications with version control
    — Core training environment
    — Common tools
    — Ease of use
    — One browser
    — Remote access
    — Streamlined processes
2. Decentralized working environment (offices)
3. Enhanced productivity
4. Information efficiencies
    — Easier access
    — Faster access
    — Increase in accuracy
    — Increase in availability
    — Increase in communication
    — Increase in resources

      — Increase in timeliness

      — Just-in-time

      — More marketing data

      — More technical sources

      — Quicker data transfer

5. Opportunities for

      — New roles

      — New skills or enhancements

6. Reductions in

      — Documentation costs

      — Duplicative resources

      — Mailing costs

      — Ordering time

      — Printing costs

      — Search effort time

      — Software distribution

      — Support costs

      — Telephone support costs

People are fearful of technology or very uncomfortable with its impact on their job status. This is the place to emphasize ease of use and access, commonality, availability of training, and the opportunities for more informational resources. The starting points you might use to resolve technological resistance are:

- Common environment

      — Common tools

      — Ease of use

- — Remote access
- — Streamlined processes
- Decentralized working environment (offices)
- Enhanced productivity
- Information efficiencies
  - — Easier access
  - — Faster access
  - — Increase in accuracy
  - — Increase in availability
  - — Increase in communication
  - — Increase in resources
  - — Increase in timeliness
  - — Just-in-time
  - — More marketing data
  - — More technical sources
  - — Quicker data transfer
- Reductions in
  - — Documentation costs
  - — Printing costs
  - — Search effort time
  - — Telephone support costs

ON THE CD-ROM

1. 13Overview.ppt—Chapter Overview
2. 13Selling.doc—Selling Skills Self-Assessment

Section 4

Customers and Vendors and an IT Project

$\mathbf{B}$ecause of the networking environment the IT manager's activities are usually managed using a project to solve a customer's need with a team. In fact very few corporate IT activities are purely an individual effort. This section addresses two important people-management concerns for any IT project: the team and customer involvement.

In Chapter 14, you develop knowledge about the skills needed for working with the customer. The essential requirement is to establish a set of measurable goals agreed upon by all parties.

In Chapter 15, you develop knowledge about the skills required to work with vendors. Even an established vendor relationship may change because of a project's goals.

CHAPTER 14

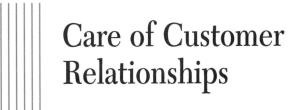

Care of Customer Relationships

Objectives: At the end of this chapter, you will be able to:

- Answer the question "What is a customer?"

- State seven skill categories of customer negotiation.

- Ask ten questions from the customer's view about you as an IT manager.

- Place the customer always first.

- Treat the customer as a stakeholder.

- Handle customer expectations caused by your actions.

- Manage customer acceptance as a process rather than as an event.

- Identify nine quality keys.

- Manage five types of project risks the customer could cause.

- Prepare customer presentations based on an essential principle.

- Identify the importance of customer views.

- Identify how the three management levels may be involved with customers.

In this chapter, you develop knowledge about the skills needed when working with the customer. A basic requirement when working with a customer on a specific project is to establish a series of measurable goals agreed upon by all parties. Any skill set used with a customer is based on these principles:

- The customer is a stakeholder in a project.

- For a project, the customer is first as long as the agreed goals are not changed without the customer comprehending the results and consequences of change.

- For day-to-day operations the customer is correct except when the customer's position is contrary to stated measurable corporate IT standards.

- The customer should be actively involved when appropriate throughout a relationship (a project).

NOTE:

Before reading this chapter, you should take the Customer Awareness Skills Self-Assessment found on the CD-ROM (14Cust.doc). An example of the self-assessment is also found in Chapter 23.

WHAT IS A CUSTOMER?

A customer is anyone other than you in the broadest of terms. More specifically in day-to-day operations it is anyone who requires IT assistance in accordance with the corporate statement or mission. For a project, the customer is the one who defines the original set of project goals and the one who must be negotiated with when there are changes to these goals. A skill most IT managers must learn is how to handle the possibility that everyone in the corporation or company is a customer. This skill is really the book's focus.

SEVEN SKILL CATEGORIES FOR CUSTOMER NEGOTIATION

The initial customer negotiation sets the tone for future relations. (See Chapter 11 for more on negotiating.) The following seven skill categories assist you in developing a well-oiled relationship:

- Know your customer.

- Listen to the customer.

- Talk on neutral ground.

- Be clear on your capabilities.

- Neither force nor be forced.

- Respond to issues in a timely manner.

- Establish the criteria of excellence.

The customer appreciates if you have taken time prior to entering the meeting to try to comprehend the customer's position. For example, you have analyzed your historical IT data for this group and can give a summary of data relevant to the item under discussion. If there are no data, you should at least look at the group's organizational chart.

You should listen to what the customer has to say; perhaps the real need is not the perceived one. The customer may say they need some specific hardware or software change to the informational system when the issue may be only a need to clarify an expectation of the IT network. Do not get into a confrontational mode. You should listen before speaking.

The meeting should be held in a neutral location. People seem threatened when negotiating or even just discussing anything while in the domain of either party.

You should state your capabilities in the meeting as to known data. Express a willingness to revise your position based on any new data. You need to express to the customer your IT process for change to the networking environment. This lets the customer know that you manage according to purpose and direction for any situation. (Perception is everything, not reality.)

An important part of this discussion deals with the question "Is this project viable?" You need to know if the customer is dreaming or ready to act. You need to know the amount of approved funding that exists. If there is none, then you need to make it clear to the customer that this is only a fact-finding meeting.

In addition, it is important to state the basic characteristics of your IT management process without going into details. At least state that you think a project, as distinct from day-to-day work, includes:

- Specific start and end dates

- Specific allocation of resources (skills, equipment, and materials)

- Measurable goals

- Organized process to meet the customer's defined goals

- Specific team involvement

Success is achieved through compromise, not through force. Each party has expectations. Each party should walk away with a set of measurable goals and with a sense of a win-win condition.

When you state that you will follow up by a given date, do so. If you delay, that reflects that you cannot manage your time. In addition, trust flies out the window. If you cannot meet your commitments in the small things, will you meet your commitments in the large things?

In conclusion, not the least in importance, you need to demonstrate what your criteria are for excellence. When appropriate you could summarize that your IT operational structure is based on independent standards and benchmarks.

Customer's View of You as the IT Manager

Any relationship has at least two sides. You have a view of the customer, but the customer has a view of you also. You have to consider that you have to present yourself not only as IT competent, but as managerially competent. Always consider yourself in a competitive position. You must present yourself favorably to the customer in these ten areas:

1. Does IT have the resource capabilities to complete work on time and on budget?

2. Does IT have the technical capabilities to complete the project satisfactorily?

3. Does IT have an organized process that represents a standard of excellence?

4. What kinds of relationships have been established with other customers by this IT manager?

5. Does the IT process fit with my expenditure capabilities?

6. Are there other offers that can achieve my goals better?

7. What advantages do I have from using this IT manager?

8. How do the results of this project enhance my marketing position?

9. Does the pricing strategy meet my financial goals for this project?

10. Does the IT manager's upper management give its support?

Place the Customer First

You have to always place the customer first as long as it is rational and makes good business sense (meets the corporate financial benchmarks or standards). You need to comprehend the customer's expectations, perspectives, and positions.

You have to recognize that for a project the customer is doing the funding. Have you and the project team given the customer the "bang" for the "buck?" Project success usually results in customer satisfaction and perhaps future opportunities. Customer satisfaction is the best type of public relations.

This does not mean the customer gets any change that is mentioned. You should have a change order process for resolving this type of situation.

Part of the confusion in working with the premises in the above paragraphs is there are at least three types of customer relationships. The customer types are not "can work with," "bad," or "worse," but:

- Financial investor

- End user

- Partner (alliance or joint venture)

It is always difficult to get the members of the IT group to comprehend the differences among these three customer types. In fact, different members may have different relationships so that all three types are your customers at the same time.

TREAT THE CUSTOMER AS A STAKEHOLDER

A stakeholder is anyone with a personal stake in an IT project or the IT operational actions. If the customer is the financial contributor or is going to pay for the product created from a project, then they have the primary investment in the project. Other stakeholders are of course you, the team, the strategic manager, consultants, and vendors. Each stakeholder requires you to use the appropriate skill set at the appropriate time and place. This means you treat any type of customer accordingly. You do not just say hello in the hallway to the "paying" customer.

CUSTOMER AND AN IT PROJECT

You might simply state that any IT project is organized to achieve measurable goals within a specified duration, with allocated resources, and with a defined team. This is a valid definition but perhaps a better one would include the customer in the definition. For example, an IT project is a structured process that focuses on the customer's requirements and priorities to give the customer a quality product on time with minimum resources. This process is based on a position that the process uses measurable goals, benchmarks, and standards for design, development, testing, and implementation of the final product(s).

CUSTOMER EXPECTATIONS CAUSED BY THE IT MANAGER

You have to be aware that any action has a reaction. In this instance, beyond the initial negotiations, the reaction is the customer's expectations. To limit expectations, be consistent. Here are five types of customer expectations you can generate intentionally or unintentionally:

- Produce timely status reports.

- Do small changes without costs.

- Have an 8-to-5 work environment.

- Be visible to the customer.

- Consider the customer's perception of issues.

> **NOTE:**
>
> It is recognized that the IT group works in a 24 × 7 environment; however, this means having a "balanced" workforce rather than an "overtime" workforce. If the customer perceives that you have to do their project with extended overtime, then the conclusion might be that you do not plan well especially in the area of time management.

CUSTOMER ACCEPTANCE PROCESS

A big mistake you can make is to think that the customer will accept the final product or operational solution without questions. Customer acceptance is a selling process. Customer involvement results in an evolving comprehension of the results.

One way to achieve customer acceptance is to have an exemplary quality control program. Nine quality keys that lead to customer satisfaction and acceptance include the following:

- Quality demonstrates an awareness of customer needs.

- Quality equates to control.

- Quality is commitment.

- Quality is measurable.

- Quality is support for the effort even when there are disagreements.

- Quality means avoidance of costs for things unnecessary.

- Quality means having the right skill at the right place at the right time.

- Quality means there is some form of communications between you and the customer. Communications can establish a bond of confidence.

- Quality requires metrics so analysis can be done to determine degree of success.

CUSTOMER INVOLVEMENT AND RISKS

You have to recognize the risks caused by your team and the customer. A risk is a potential event that could cause serious detriment to the project process such as major unexpected costs in time or resources. You need to be prepared to handle these customer-generated risks:

- Financial support becomes unavailable.

- Customer is not participating in agreed-upon reviews.

- Response time to questions is not timely.

- Seems to have new interpretations of goals.

- Skill resources availability degrades.

PREPARE CUSTOMER PRESENTATIONS

There are many ways to present information visually. Chapter 18 covers in more detail the design and development of presentations. The essential principle in developing customer presentations is to state performance as to cost, time, and the measurable goals. Do no get into the technical details. You lose your customer this way so quickly you will not have to blink twice.

If you have half an hour to present, limit the slides so you talk for no more than 20 minutes. This means a maximum of a dozen slides with no more than three bulleted items per slide. You do not talk for the whole half hour and then take questions. This type of action reflects on your ability to manage time well.

USE GOLDEN OPPORTUNITIES

There may be many things the customer looks at, but only a few are important. Here is where the gold is:

- Customer's comfort with the technology

- Your commitment to schedule

- Your consistency

- Cost equals performance

- Excellent line of communication

- Your flexibility when required

- Measurable objectives

- Your IT organized management process

- Right people in the right place at the right time

- Your upper management supports you

MANAGEMENT INVOLVEMENT

Each of the manager types has a clear responsibility in customer involvement. The strategic manager is the corporation spokesperson; the tactical manager, you, are the IT spokesperson; and the operational managers should adhere to the IT goals until they receive an official change order.

There are a few things you must enforce to have functional customer relations. They include the following:

- The strategic manager should not make decisions about an IT project to a customer without prior discussion with you and you should be present when the decision is given.

- The tactical manager is the spokesperson for the project. The IT manager is not the interface to the customer unless that person is also the project manager.

- Operational managers are not to make project changes that are based on personal conversations with the customer or on personal opinions.

- The customer should be involved in the status meetings or reports generated by an IT project.

ON THE CD-ROM

1. 14Overview.ppt—Chapter Overview

2. 14Cust.doc—Customer Awareness Skills Self-Assessment

CHAPTER 15

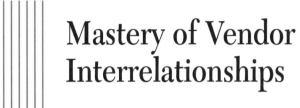

Mastery of Vendor Interrelationships

Objectives: At the end of this chapter, you will be able to:

- Answer the question, "What is a vendor?"
- Interview a vendor.
- Negotiate with a vendor.
- Manage quality control with a vendor.
- Develop vendor documentation.

In this chapter, you develop knowledge about the skills required to work with vendors and with consultants who are vendors of ideas or techniques. Even an established vendor relationship may change because of a project's goals. Whether you use a vendor to assist in solving one of your customer's problems or you use the vendor to assist in solving an IT problem, you are the customer in the relationship.

It does happen on rare occasions that a well-known consulting firm or vendor can make you feel like it is the customer rather than you.

> **NOTE:**
>
> Before reading this chapter, you should take the Vendor Awareness Skills Self-Assessment. It is found on the CD-ROM (15Ven.doc) and in Chapter 23.

What Is a Vendor?

A vendor is a person or an organization that can deliver a product such as an application, materials, equipment, or skills to achieve a goal in a manner that is timely, effective, and efficient. A special type of vendor is a consultant. A consultant works with ideas, techniques, or processes that are educational or informational.

Selecting Vendors

One of the first things you might do for a major project is acquire consultants or bring in local IT support vendors. Before acquiring the consultants or vendors, establish the criteria for their selection. This is the type of information you should get from them before they grace your doors:

- Development, design, maintenance, and support levels available

- Rates

- References from where they have done similar work

- Resumes with emphasis on experiences related to the project's goals

- Security solution knowledge level when applicable

> **NOTE:**
>
> Feel free to ask a vendor to give you customized resumes on its consultants that reflect your project goal requirements. The resume is discussed in Chapter 3.

It has been said that it takes only thirty seconds to evaluate an individual's resume. Take a bit longer to evaluate a vendor's resume. However, as with an individual's resume, you should have a checklist based on the answers developed to create the job description. First, you need to decide the number of check marks the resume must have before further consideration. Second, you must decide if certain items must have a check mark before further consideration.

INTERVIEWING A VENDOR

Once a vendor has passed the selection hurdle, you need to interview the vendor and present an issue that you think you are going to have. Then ask them for their ideas and suggestions. Do the same thing with all candidates so you can evaluate their solutions and your comfort zone.

In fact, to enhance the interview process, you might call all vendors at the same time and give a presentation on your needs. (See Chapter 18 for a discussion on presentations.) All vendors have the same information that is given in the same manner. Thus, all responses from the vendors should be given in the context of the presentation.

Chapter 3 discusses details on interviewing and hiring skills. The basic premise to be used is that in the interview of representatives from a vendor treat the action as though you were interviewing an individual. You should look for consistency in answers and for facts rather than descriptive sales information.

As in the individual interview process, you need to:

- Define the skill requirements.
- Assess the vendor's "resume" or credentials.
- Write questions for an interview.
- Follow a formal interview process.
- Use a team for the interview.
- Follow-up on the interview.

You should use measurable criteria. The vendor should give you measurable solutions. Has the vendor prepared for the interview as well or better than an individual would?

One area of expertise is the technical support of the vendor that has a product that you need to achieve a project goal. They should have historical data as to the amount of time it took to install and configure their product into another system. If they do not have this type of data then immediately look somewhere else for another solution.

NEGOTIATING WITH A VENDOR

You should negotiate with a vendor as you would with one of your customers. You should seek a "win-win" situation.

The skills of negotiation are discussed in Chapter 11. What are the basic skills in negotiating with a vendor? The skill set includes:

- Define one's requirements, needs, or desires

- Define the issues

- Determine what can be traded

- Establish an offense and defense

- Hold with one's principles

The negotiating skill set should be based on the awareness required to manage negotiation dynamics. First, become aware of the attitudes of negotiators as to the win-win situation. Second, know how your personality might affect the decision-making process. Third, know your abilities to do problem solving. Fourth, be aware of the organizational dynamics involved in the negotiations. Fifth, define the negotiating boundary by which all work is to be done. Sixth, determine the resources required for achieving successful results. Seventh and finally, develop a decision that all members will support.

MANAGING QUALITY CONTROL WITH A VENDOR

When does this activity begin? It begins while you are negotiating with the vendor. You should establish the benchmarks and standards by which the results of the vendor will be evaluated during the negotiations, not after approval of the contract. This type of action is actually a change to the contract.

In the case of a project, the vendor should be bound by the quality control and assurance process established by the project team. In the case of a special IT effort, the vendor should meet your process.

The first skill set of quality control is to comprehend the basics of the process. There are two basic components of the quality process, assurance and control. Quality, as defined by those of the profession, is "conformance to specification." Another way to state the purpose of the quality process is that it seeks to minimize performance errors.

Assurance is based on performance. It is the establishing of performance standards, then measuring and evaluating project performance against these standards. Finally, assurance acts on performance deviations.

Control acts to meet the standards through the gathering of performance information, inspecting, monitoring, and testing.

The essential word is "performance." This means the project activities should be evaluated against the following by quality assurance and control:

- Project goals
- Standards, such as ISO
- Corporate standards
- Standards established by the project team during the planning phase
- Schedule
- Budget

Quality assurance and control can affect a number of areas including:

- Customer satisfaction
- Design improvement
- Development improvement

- Implementation integrity
- Testing guaranty

> **NOTE:**
>
> Where *standards* is used above, it could be *standards and benchmarks.*

A second skill is the ability to identify potential errors. With a vendor, you may have to keep a more direct watch or ensure that you have a quality control cadre that can handle this matter. There are many sources for errors. Most are found in the general operational process. Twenty errors are:

1. Activity sequencing in error
2. Coding error
3. Database format error
4. Documentation error
5. Equipment is below standards
6. Failure to give timely reports
7. Feature not a part of a project goal
8. Hardware incompatibility
9. Material does not meet standards
10. Network component incompatibility
11. Not using appropriate standards
12. Operating system incompatibility to system infrastructure
13. Project activity not one defined in the schedule
14. Report layout in error
15. Requirement specification in error

16. Resource received is not in accordance with specification

17. Skill level is not valid

18. Software incompatibility

19. Training objectives do not meet a project goal

20. Vendor product incompatibility to system

Ensuring Required Vendor Documentation

The customer has a new application. The customer does not know how to start the application. What is missing? There needs to be basic user-friendly application documentation from the vendor. The information should not be wrapped in technical jargon. There should be a short user guide and a longer more comprehensive guide. As with most things, eighty percent of the people will use twenty percent of the features. Twenty percent of the users need the comprehensive guide, but they do not want to read it.

For a project, you need a number of documents, but from a vendor you need three document types whether it is for a customer or operational project. These three documents are:

- Business Affiliate Plan

- Third-Party Marketing Agreement

- Third-Party Service Plan

The Business Affiliate Plan provides information when the project is to be developed by a third-party developer. The plan might consist of the following:

- Explanation for the need for a third-party developer

- How the third party doing the development qualifies

- What part the third party plays in the marketing program

- Training requirements
- Documentation requirements
- Quality control system description

The Third-Party Marketing Agreement provides the plans where the project is to be developed by a third-party developer. This agreement may include:

- Product content
- Delivery schedules
- Marketing strategy
- Verification strategy
- Documentation strategy
- Training strategy

The Third-Party Service Plan provides how the project is to be serviced by a third-party developer. The question is, "Will the third party do customer service?" The plan may include details on:

- Customer training
- Customer documentation
- Diagnostic tools
- Support process

ON THE CD-ROM

1. 15Overview.ppt—Chapter Overview
2. 15Ven.doc—Vendor Awareness Skills Self-Assessment

Section 5

Communication Skills

This section describes two ways in which we communicate, oral and written, and then looks at an environment where we do both; the presentation. Body language is a part of oral language. There are other ways to communicate but are not usually a part of IT project management, such as art and music. The exception to this statement is of course electronic gaming development.

Chapter 16 focuses on the skills to speak in an effective and efficient manner.

Chapter 17 focuses on the skills to write in an effective and efficient manner.

In Chapter 18, the reader acquires knowledge for the skills to develop and give effective and efficient presentations.

CHAPTER 16

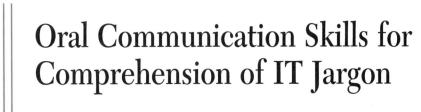

Oral Communication Skills for Comprehension of IT Jargon

Objectives: At the end of this chapter, you will be able to:

- Do a self-assessment of feedback skills.

- State the importance of why you should not use jargon.

- Explain the danger of ambiguity in oral communication.

- Give five techniques for effective communication.

- Evaluate your oral communication skills.

- Give rules for managing a meeting.

- Be aware that one person's *byte* is another person's *bite*.

- Summarize oral communication skills.

This chapter focuses on the skills to communicate orally, that is to speak, in an effective and efficient manner. Remember what you say must be perceived by the audience as being truthful. Truth is transmitted from speaker to audience when the communication is accepted by the audience on a physical level of observation and a logical level of abstraction. You need to recognize that when you speak, it is probably accepted on an emotional level and even perhaps a spiritual (non-religious idea here) level, more so than an intellectual level. This statement is important because when you use too much IT jargon that is not comprehensible to your audience, you have not communicated with them. The speech is a monologue, not a dialog.

NOTE:

Do the Oral Communication Skills Self-Assessment (16Communicate.doc on the CD-ROM and found in Chapter 23) prior to reading this chapter.

IMPORTANCE OF NOT USING JARGON

When you have a fondness for speaking IT jargon remember what happened at the Tower of Babel; there was noise and confusion. The builders could no longer communicate with each other. They were no longer one people, but groups of people each with a common set of words. There was no comprehension among all the people.

You need to communicate effectively to coordinate your own work and that of others. You have to make an explicit effort in your conversation so you will have communication. If you do not do this, your work will collapse through misunderstanding and error.

The point is to treat any critical conversation as you would any other managed activity by establishing a goal, planning what to say, and checking afterwards that you have achieved that goal by summarizing the conversation. This is the golden road to working effectively with others in building through a common effort.

BASIC ORAL COMMUNICATION SKILLS

Communication is best achieved through simple planning and control. This position is specifically valid at meetings, where conversations need particular care. Most conversations sort of drift along; in business, this is a waste. As a manager, you need to seek communication rather than babble. For an efficient and effective conversation, there are three considerations:

- Make your message heard.

- Comprehend the intended message sent to you.

- Control the flow of the communication.

You must learn to listen as well as to speak. This is not a platitude; the message is hugely significant to your effectiveness as a manager. If you do not explicitly develop the skill of listening, you may not hear the information or suggestion, which enhance the perceptions of you as a manager. Perhaps the highest compliment that can be paid to you as a manager is not that you speak well, but that you listen well.

AMBIGUITY LEADS TO MORE BABBLE

When you use IT jargon you produce ambiguity in your audience. The ambiguity error in computer science is a gross error caused by imprecise synchronism, such as in an analog-to-digital conversion. I do not need a computer to produce ambiguity even with an IT manager who thinks everyone should speak in bits and bytes. It is very appropriate to say here, "What we've got here is failure to communicate."

As a manager your view of words should be pragmatic (basic, practical, or businesslike) rather than theoretical (conceptual, academic, or not applicable). Thus, words do not mean what the dictionary states; rather they do mean what the hearer hears.

Suppose you give an instruction, which contains an ambiguity that is not noticed and the consequence is the wrong product is produced. Who is at fault? We have a failure of communication. Time has been wasted, the product is delayed and you have an unhappy customer.

Attributing blame may produce short-term satisfaction, but it does not address the problem. In everything you say or hear, you must look out for a possible lack of understanding and the need to clarify the ambiguity.

The greatest source of difficulty is that words often have different meanings depending upon context, culture, or misuse of words. I did a book on translations in telephony. Do you know what the subject was? It was concerned with what the pressing of the digits on the keypad did on first occurrence. You know that pressing the digit 1 signifies to the code that a long distance call has to be handled. The point here is that "translation" in this instance has absolutely nothing to do with translating a document from English to French or French to English.

If you recognize that there is a potential misunderstanding, you must stop the conversation and ask for the valid interpretation. Again, if you do not understand, ask for clarification.

A second problem is that people simply make mistakes. Your job is not only to spot ambiguities, but also to counter inconsistencies. For example, in thinking over several alternatives you might have a momentary confusion and say one of them while meaning another. You have to be aware of the potential problem and counteract it.

A third problem is the sin of omission, a word was not heard. The omission of a simple word can be devastating. How important is the word "not"?

We now have ambiguity, misstatement, and omission. What do you do to save the day?

- Confirm verbally.
- Confirm in writing
- State context.

PRACTICAL SKILLS TO EFFECTIVE COMMUNICATION

As with all effective communication, you should decide in advance on the purpose of a conversation and the plan for success. How many people have you met who are truly proficient at "thinking on their feet?" The following are a few techniques to assist in the conversation:

- Be assertive
- Be professional
- Assume you might be in error

- Seek information
- Let others speak

To be assertive is "to declare; state clearly." This is your goal. If someone argues against you, even loses their temper, you should be quietly assertive. To be assertive means to have a three-step action plan:

- Acknowledge in some manner that you comprehend the other person's position.
- State your own point of view clearly and concisely.
- State what you want to happen next.

When you have a confrontation, be professional by not losing your self-control because, simply, it serves no use (a lose-lose situation). You must be consistent and fair so that your staff knows where they stand. If you deliberately lose your temper for effect, know your decision is never heard.

Before you criticize, assume that you have misunderstood the situation. Ask questions first which check the other person's view of the situation. This simple courtesy will save you grief.

You can ask either a closed or an open question. A closed question usually means you are seeking a reply such as "yes," "no," or "maybe." An open question hands over the speaking role to someone else and forces the person to say something that hopefully is informative. Open questions are extremely easy to ask. You establish the goal of the question and then you start the sentence with the words: what, when, which, how, or why.

There are many forms of flattery. The most effective is to show people your interest. One way to express interest besides nodding your head is to ask questions. Silence can be misunderstood. Here are three example questions:

- What do you think about the idea?
- Have you ever run into this problem?
- How would you resolve this issue?

ORAL COMMUNICATION IN MEETINGS

In any organization, "meetings" play a vital part in the flow of information. They act as a mechanism for gathering resources and pooling them for a common objective. They are disliked and mocked because they are usually ineffective, dull, time wasting, and annoying. Your challenge is to break this mold and to make your meetings effective. A significant part of planning for an effective meeting is planning the meeting's communication.

A meeting is the ultimate form of managed conversation. You should organize the information and structure of the meeting to support the effective communication of the participants. Meetings do not have to be formal to be effective, but they have to be decisive. People value efficiency and want to know that their contribution will be heard.

Planning for a meeting requires you to answer a few questions:

- Should you cancel?

- Who should attend?

- How long should the meeting be?

- What should be on the agenda?

- How shall the meeting be conducted?

- How is communication to be managed?

- What are the rules of conduct for the meeting?

- How should various types of responses be handled?

You must first ask, as with all conversations, is it worth your time? If the meeting involves the interchange of views and the communication of the status of related projects, then you should have a meeting. Should you have a meeting to discuss the schedules for reviews?

You must be strict as to who attends a meeting. A meeting loses its effectiveness if too many people are involved. If someone comes and has no useful function, the person still wants to speak and has no relevant input.

It may seem difficult to predict the length of a discussion. It is best to start on time and end on time using a distributed agenda with time allocations. Enforce the agenda. After a few such meetings, speakers will be more decisive. There is no communication where there was to be a one-hour meeting that turns into three hours. You need to stress the meeting's timeline and thus force the pace of the discussion. Perhaps you can use a statement such as "This is what we have to achieve, this is how long we have to get it done."

If an unexpected point arises, you have to realize that since it is unexpected there is a problem that the right people are not present or you do not have the necessary information. If the new discussion looks likely to take time, stop the discussion and deal with the agreed agenda. The new topic should then be handled at another meeting.

The purpose of an agenda is to inform participants of the subject of the meeting in advance, and to structure the discussion at the meeting itself. You should circulate a draft agenda to inform people beforehand and to solicit ideas. Before the meeting, you should send a revised agenda with enough time for people to prepare. If you know in advance that a particular participant either needs information or will be providing information, then make this clear so that there is no confusion.

The agenda states the purpose of each section and its allocated time for the meeting. There can be a stated expectation from each section. The goal of the meeting should be sufficiently precise that it can be summarized and displayed for all interested parties to see.

Whether you are the chair or not, as the manager you must provide the necessary support to coordinate the contributions of the participants. The degree of control that you exercise over the meeting can vary throughout. If you prepared, the meeting can effectively run itself.

You can maintain communication in a meeting using three important tools beyond the ones already given. They are the following:

- Clarification

- Summary

- Focus on stated goals

In any meeting, it is possible to begin the proceedings by establishing a code of conduct. Thus if the group contains opinionated "lions" (they love to roar), you might all agree that all contributions should be limited to two minutes. You can then limit babble with the full backing of the group. A fundamental rule of conduct is: "No one should be laughed at or dismissed."

The stated purpose of a meeting may suggest to you a specific way of conducting it. In addition, each section might be conducted differently. For instance, if the purpose is to convey information, the meeting might begin with a formal presentation (discussed in Chapter 18) followed by questions. However, a meeting that is to seek information would start with a precise statement of the topic and then an open discussion supported by notes on a display, or a formal brainstorming session to make a decision. There might be a review of the alternatives, a definition of the criteria to be applied, and a plan for how the decision is to be reached.

Preparing for a meeting includes preparing responses to various types of comments. The following is just a sampling of responses to comments:

- If a participant strays from the agenda item, call the participant back to the agenda by saying "We should deal with that at another meeting, but what do you feel about the agenda item X?"

- If a point is too vague, ask for greater clarity: "What exactly do you have in mind?"

- If people chat, you might either simply state your difficulty in hearing the speaker, or ask them, "What do you think about that point?"

- If someone interrupts, you should suggest that: "We can hear your point after X has finished."

- If the speaker begins to ramble, wait for a pause and then say, "I understand your point, does anyone disagree?"

- If there is an error, look for a good point first and then say, "I see how that would work if it was that, but what would happen if it is this?"

- If there is confusion, you might ask, "Do I hear correctly that you said . . . ?"

- If you disagree, be very specific by saying "I disagree because . . ."

- If you do not understand, say, "I do not understand that, would you explain your point a little more; or do you mean A or Z?"

ON THE CD-ROM

1. 16Overview.ppt—Chapter Overview

2. 16Communicate.doc—Oral Communication Skills Self-Assessment

CHAPTER 17

Written Communication Skills
for Everyone

Objectives: At the end of this chapter, you will be able to:

- Answer the question, "Does your method of writing reflect you?"

- Explain the golden rule of written communication: Do not use words that might be misinterpreted easily.

- State reasons for writing clear technical documents.

- Identify purposes for writing.

- Give steps to productive writing.

- Evaluate your written communication skills.

> **NOTE:**
>
> Before reading this chapter, you should take the Written Communication Skills Self-Assessment. It is found in Chapter 23 and on the CD-ROM as 17Communicate.doc.

This chapter focuses on the skills needed to write in an effective and efficient manner. You may have heard the rule that you should write as you speak; forget it. IT professionals cannot write to other functional groups as they speak to each other. Actually, this is true of those functional groups also. What is required is to write in a common language. It is just a harder task for IT professionals. You do not demonstrate your intelligence by saying, "There are a plethora of problems that programmers can resolve." (Do not run to your dictionary, *plethora* here means excessive or too many.) Surprise your audience and get their attention by writing so they can comprehend exactly what you have written.

Words as a Reflection of You

Remember, what you write must be perceived by the audience as being truthful. Truth is transmitted from writer to reader(s) when the communication is accepted by the audience on a physical level of observation and a logical level of abstraction. You need to recognize that when you write, it is probably accepted on an emotional level and even perhaps on a spiritual level (this does not mean religious level), more so than on an intellectual level. This statement is important because when you use too much IT jargon that is not comprehensible to your readers you have not communicated with them. The document is a one-way and a non-interactive statement.

NOTE:

Interactive here means an immediate response that happens in the spoken word. Time gives what you thought was a bloom the opportunity to turn into poison ivy.

WRITTEN TECHNICAL JARGON CAN BE MORE NIGHT THAN LIGHT

Writing is an essential skill required for a successful manager, engineer, or programmer. Jargon can lead to confusion rather than insight. To an IT manager this may be obvious when working with other functional groups. However, even with the IT group one has to be careful of jargon, especially acronyms. You say, "We need to use POP." It is clear to you that you mean *Post Office Protocol;* however, it also means *Point of Presence.* You would expect others to understand what you have written because of the context of the document. What you expect and what actually happens can be two very different situations. This obviously becomes more complex in an IT proposal for a project for one or more functional groups. Will such words as "firewall" or "gateway" be technically clear to your audience?

The most significant point about technical (computer or engineering) writing is that it is totally different from the writing most people were taught. You have to recognize and comprehend the difference or your writing will always miss the mark.

IMPORTANCE OF TECHNICAL WRITING

Writing is the major means of communication within an organization. Writing can be on paper or in electronic format. An IT manager has to be concerned with writing project proposals and clarifying issues with e-mails.

Because of the general business environment, writing may be the major product of an IT professional. You should keep a log for a couple of weeks and determine the percentage for yourself. The figure will probably be around thirty percent of your time. It is vital for you to develop the skill of productive writing for three reasons. First, if thirty percent of your time is involved in writing it has to be productive or you will get further and further behind in trying to handle your management plate. Second, the success of your projects will depend upon it. Third, since so much of the communication between you and upper management occurs in writing, your whole career may depend on its quality.

Writing has two major goals. First, for both writer and reader it clarifies. Second, it conveys information. If neither goal is met, your document is not productive. In relation to a project, documentation must provide a means to clarify and explain project status, and to prepare for the next stages. However, in a single event effective and efficient writing is critical. The minutes of a meeting form a permanent and definitive record. Think how many times well written minutes can resolve an interpersonal issue.

Good writing causes the writer and the reader to focus. Quality is improved since writing clarifies product design. It forces the designer to consider and explore more fully a design concept. A large and successful telecommunications corporation uses design documents with peer reviews to eliminate many potential bugs before any coding begins.

You might see the rough edges of an idea by writing it down on a page or, since you are on the cutting edge of technology, use an electronic word processor. When you write down "The problem is X" you have to ensure that the statement clarifies and gives you information at the same time. X might actually only be smoke rather than the fire.

PURPOSES FOR WRITING

IT professionals write for very distinct and restricted purposes, which are achieved through simplicity. Few technical documents become great works of literature. An IT document is primarily designed to convey and clarify information, not to entertain. In addition, the document should be written so it can sell an idea. A fundamental skill of a writer of an IT document is to extract the significant data and support it with a minimal argument. You might say your job is to filter out the noise.

There are specific situations for writing. Purposes for writing have been given in most of the chapters. You have to use effective and efficient writing when you do interviewing, motivating, reviewing, organizing, negotiating, facilitating, and presenting.

Basic Steps for Writing

Remember the goals of writing are to clarify and inform. Next, do the following six steps:

- Define your goal.

- Consider the reader.

- Develop a logical structure.

- Draft the text.

- Edit the text.

- Revise the text.

You start with your goal. Every document should have a specific reason for being written. If there is no productive reason for writing, there should not be a document.

Next, decide what the reader wants and how it should be said. You should select and state the requirements precisely and concisely. There are three considerations:

- Identify what the reader knows.

- Identify what the reader needs to know.

- Identify the order and emphasis of the message.

If you are writing on the same subject to two or more functional groups, you might have as many different documents. Do not try to write one document that includes all the audiences unless it is information that all should have.

Structure is used to present the information so that it is more accessible to the reader. Remember we live in the age of the commercial, or the age of the short attention span. You need to provide the information in small manageable bites. The document's structure can assist you in this process. All you need to do is perform a hierarchical decomposition. The guidelines are:

- Have distinct sections.

- Have distinct paragraphs for each section.

- Have one idea per paragraph.

- Have precise supporting information in each paragraph.

- Use graphics when better than text.

The power of a written communication over oral communication is that you have the opportunity to draft, revise and edit what you are going to say. Never forget revising and editing. A published book opportunity was lost because the publisher said, "Send the draft for structure," and unfortunately the reviewers were more concerned with content. Twelve things you should be checking for to be sure that they help to clarify and inform the document are the following:

- Layout (simple structure)

- Style (language accessibility)

- The beginning (You succeed here or you lose here.)

- Punctuation

- Spelling

- Simple errors (to, too, two)

- Sentence length

- Word length

- Incorrect word

- Jargon

- Wordiness

- The conclusion (last opportunity to succeed)

ON THE CD-ROM

1. 17Overview.ppt—Chapter Overview

2. 17Communicate.doc—Written Communication Skills Self-Assessment

CHAPTER 18

Presentation Skills for IT Team Unification

Objectives: At the end of this chapter, you will be able to:

- Answer the question, "What is a presentation?"

- State basic skills for developing a presentation.

- Answer the question, "What can a presentation do for you?"

- List objectives for a presentation.

- Develop a "selling an idea" presentation.

- Develop an informational presentation.

- Develop a "newspaper" type presentation.

- Develop the "sandwich" presentation.

- State principles for a visual presentation.

- State basic rules for delivering a presentation.

- Discuss the importance of a self-evaluation for a presentation.

- Identify basic requirements for an upper management presentation.

- Identify eleven important intangibles that reflect successful presentation skills.

NOTE:

Before reading this chapter, you should do the Presentation Skills Self-Assessment. It is found in Chapter 23 and on the CD-ROM as 18Present.doc.

In this chapter, you acquire knowledge for the skills to develop and give effective and efficient presentations. Authority, enthusiasm, and animation should be used equally. The required self-control and discipline to be effective comes from practice and professional guidance.

WHAT IS A PRESENTATION?

A presentation is the merging of oral and written skills to state effectively a goal that should be comprehended by your audience in the same way you comprehend it. You say that you are only going to speak, so why do you have to be concerned with writing skills? Unless you are going to chatter off the tip of your tongue, you have to make at least a written outline or a script of the speech.

Management is the science and art of getting things done. A presentation is the science and art of using a fast and potentially effective method of getting things done through others. A presentation is a formal method for bringing people together to plan, monitor, and review progress. A presentation can be used to sell an idea or a need. A presentation can establish a "comfort zone" for your customers and upper management.

A presentation is more than putting some words into a PowerPoint template. It is to know your audience, your subject, and yourself.

WHAT IS THE BASIC PRESENTATION PROCESS?

There are many steps in the presentation, including those steps for good oral and written communication discussed in Chapters 16 and 17. Some of the basic steps in the presentation process include:

1. Identify the problems and implementation of the solutions.

2. Get personal feedback from experienced presenters.

3. Prepare material.

   — Set the objectives and expectations (knowledge level and presentation time).

   — Do a detailed analysis of the audience.

   — Ensure the material matches the audience's needs.

   — Gather and select the vital information.

   — Structure the presentation design to give form and clarity.

   — Compile and work from a script or notes.

   — Search for the right words and eliminate the IT jargon.

4. Deliver the material.

   — Use a personal style.

   — Speak with power and persuasion using language the audience can comprehend.

   — Control speaking stress, fear, and apprehension. (Do not use "okay" as a pause.)

   — Seek inner calm and outward composure. (You are the expert.)

   — Make a visual impact using posture, movement, or gestures.

   — Command attention by using an expressive voice.

   — Communicate the message.

— Handle the questions by listening.

— Become aware of areas that require further development and improvement.

WHAT CAN A PRESENTATION DO FOR YOU?

The impact of your presentation on your audience is your first priority. However, a presentation has *two* sides, the audience and you. Some of the impacts of a presentation on you include:

- It allows you to ask questions and to initiate discussion on issues important to you.

- It can show evidence of decisive planning so the audience will become confident in your position.

- It gives you the opportunity to perform.

- It puts you on display.

- The audience can become motivated to undertake the ideas or tasks that you are presenting.

- The audience can become persuaded of the merits of your ideas and provide any necessary support.

- The audience might become impressed by your skills and abilities so they can provide resources (especially for upper management).

OBJECTIVES OF THE PRESENTATION

To achieve the objectives of a presentation means you have to be prepared and organized. The essential objectives are:

- Have a positive reception through effective transmission.

- Have a presentation geared to the audience, not the speaker.

- The audience needs to comprehend the message.

- The presentation has to express the value of the presented idea.

- The message of the presentation should be remembered.

It is imperative to plan your beginning carefully; there are six elements:

- Handle administrative duties.

- Get the audience's attention.

- Establish a theme.

- Present a structure.

- Create empathy.

- Make a final good impression.

When planning your presentation you should make a note to find out if there are any administrative details which need to be announced at the beginning. This is practical for two reasons. First, if these details are overlooked the audience may become distracted as they wonder what is going to happen next. Second, too often the first few minutes of the presentation are lost while people adjust their coats, drift in with coffee and finish the conversation they were having with the person next to them. Thus, you can eliminate these activities happening during your presentation.

You need to get the audience's attention because you only have a limited time and every minute is precious to you. So, from the beginning, make sure they pay attention.

You need to establish a theme to start the audience thinking about the subject matter of your presentation. This can be done by a statement of your essential objective. The audience will have experiences or opinions on the objective. At the beginning, you must make them bring these experiences into their own minds.

You must present a structure so the audience will know what to expect. This can help to establish the theme and provide something concrete to hold everyone's attention. The audience should be prepared for an end.

If you create empathy, you can win the audience at the first. You should be able to keep them for the remainder of the presentation. You should plan exactly how you wish to appear and use the opening to establish the relationship. You need to decide the role and establish it at the very beginning.

The final impression you make on the audience is the one they will remember. Prepare your closure with great care. The ending is equal in importance to the beginning. A serious error is to tell the audience that this is the summary because at that point they simply switch off. The end should come unexpectedly with a vital phrase that leaves a lasting memory.

DEVELOPING A "SELLING AN IDEA" PRESENTATION

The first step in preparing a presentation is to define a precise objective, preferably measurable. This should be a simple, concise statement of intent. For example, the purpose of your speech may be to obtain funds for X. Next, you should add the amount and the duration of the spending.

The second step is to determine how many different objectives you can achieve in the allocated time. It will be fewer than you expect initially. It is far more productive to succeed with one goal than to fail with several. It is best to have an essential objective and perhaps two associated lesser objectives, providing they do not distract from the essential one. You should focus, focus, and focus.

The third step is to consider the audience to determine how best to achieve your objective in the context of these people. You need to know their language and aims while attending your presentation. The ideas in the presentation should appear to be the ideas of the audience. Reception, perhaps that is perception, is everything. You need to emphasize solutions to the concerns of the audience.

The fourth step is to prepare an opening remark that shows you comprehend their problem. You want to get the audience's attention at the beginning. You are a salesperson of an idea. The idea of being a salesperson is discussed in more detail in Chapter 13. If you show comprehension of the audience's problem and you have a solution, then the audience will be flattered at your attention and they will be attentive. You are looking for nodding of heads in agreement.

The fifth step is to develop a structure for your presentation. If you do not show you are organized, how can the audience believe you are organized outside of the presentation? However, the structure must not get in the way of the message. The structure should be simple. By the way, it takes longer to design a simple structure than a complex one. If you determine a section is unnecessary to the achievement of the essential objective, cut it out.

Perhaps the simplest structure is sequential. A presentation with this structure consists of a series of linked statements ultimately leading to a conclusion. However, this simplicity can only be achieved by careful and deliberate delineation between each section. You make frequent reminders to the audience of the essential point, and explicit explanation of how the next point leads from this.

Another structure is to use a hierarchical decomposition or topic outline with the essential topic being broken down into sub-topics and each major topic into smaller topics until eventually everything is broken down into very small basic units. The danger with this structure in a presentation is the audience is restricted to your presentation order. You should summarize each section at its conclusion and introduce each major new section with a statement of how it lies in the hierarchical order.

NOTE:

Very little of what you say should be on the presentation overheads. The overheads are to speak from, not to read.

Developing an Informational Presentation

Probably more of your presentations are to explain a previous decision or to seek approval for a plan of action. In these cases, the format might be question-oriented. First, you introduce the problem and any necessary background. Second, you outline the various solutions to that problem with the advantages and disadvantages of each solution. Third, you summarize each possible option in terms of their positives and negatives. Fourth, you present the preferred solution for approval or initiate a discussion that leads to the decision. To get a desired outcome, you establish during the presentation the criteria by which the various options are to be judged.

Developing a Presentation Using the Newspaper Metaphor

To prepare for this type of presentation look at the front or editorial pages of your local newspaper. What attracts you to read a given article? A presentation can be structured in a similar manner. First, you introduce the essential point in its entirety in a catchy opening. Second, the next few "paragraphs" repeat the same information only giving additional details to each point. Third, the next section is used to develop certain themes for each point and again adding information. This is repeated until the reporter (you) runs out of story. Fourth, the editor (you) simply decides upon the points that are necessary and makes cuts accordingly. The editor includes use of space as a criterion.

There are two main advantages to this style. First, it could increase the audience's reception to the essential ideas. At every stage of the "story" the audience becomes familiar with the ideas and knows what to expect next. The hearing turns into the audience believing the ideas are their own. Second, the duration of the presentation can be easily altered by cutting the talk in exactly the same manner as the newspaper editor might have done to the news story.

Developing the "Sandwich" Presentation

Without question, the sandwich presentation is the simplest and most direct format. The rule is to summarize what you are going say, say it, and summarize what you said. The essential justification is contained in the middle in this beginning-middle-end format. It is preceded by an introduction and followed by a summary and conclusion. This is really the appropriate format for a short presentation.

Developing the Visual Component of the Presentation

The first rule is to prepare overheads to speak from, not to be read. You should have no more than three bulleted items. Second, the overheads should be readable—that is, use a large font and distinct contrasting colors. The font that is readable on a monitor is not necessarily readable in a large room. One should not use a blue background and a slightly lighter blue for the font. I have seen this used at a conference with the presentations being given by book publishers. The first rule was broken.

Most people expect visual reinforcement for any oral communication. Being an IT manager, people expect you to use presentation technologies more than other functional managers.

There are a few rules that should be followed to ensure they are used effectively. Most rules are common sense, and most are commonly ignored, such as using a large sans serif (without curves) font. The rules include the following:

- Each overhead should have a distinct purpose.

- Each overhead should be readable.

- Each overhead should be uncluttered.

- Each overhead should have words comprehensible by all.

- Use handouts to supplement overheads.

- Any graphic should be relevant to the presentation.

DELIVERY SKILLS FOR A PRESENTATION

Whatever you say or show, it is you who are the focus of the audience's attention. You have the power both to kill the message and to enhance it beyond its worth. Your goal is to use the potential of the presentation to ensure that the audience is motivated and inspired rather than dreaming or doodling. There are five basic points of the human body which deserve attention in presentation skills: the eyes, the voice, the expression, the appearance, and the body position.

The eyes are the doorway to the soul and are the most effective tool in convincing the audience of your integrity, openness, and confidence in the presentation's objectives. This impression may be false, but how it is conveyed is the reception. Any conversation is under continuous evaluation through eye contact and the body language. During the presentation, you should enhance rapport with the audience by using eye contact with each member of the audience frequently. During presentations, try to hold your gaze fixed in specific directions for no more than ten seconds at a time.

The two most important aspects of speaking are projection and variation. It is important to realize that very few people can use an ordinary conversational voice in a presentation. You need to speak slowly and to take your time. There is no constraint to maintain a constant flow. In addition, ensure that you speak slightly louder than normal. You need also to try to vary the pitch and speed of your presentation.

The audience will watch your face. If you are frowning then the audience will frown; if you smile, they will wonder why and listen to find out. The point is, make sure that your facial expressions are natural, only more so.

When it comes to appearance, use the conventions of your company. In the last analysis, this is a matter of personal choice. If the presentation is good, no one will remember what you wore. That choice should however be deliberately made; you must dress for the audience, not for yourself. Dress to improve communication, not to hinder it.

Watch a movie to see how the actors convey their message and character personalities by the way they stand. Some actors convey more through the way they stand than what they say. Thus while you are giving a presentation your stance and posture will convey a great deal about you, perhaps more than you want. The least you must do is make sure your stance expresses a positive perception. You should use your body as a dynamic tool to develop audience rapport. The big issue is what to do with your hands. The principle is to keep your hands still, except when used in conjunction with your presentation.

Self-Evaluation of a Presentation

The final step of a presentation is when it is over, you should try to objectively evaluate your performance. You can do this alone or with a friend from the audience. You need to decide what was the least successful point and resolve to concentrate on that point in the next presentation. If it is a problem associated with the preparation, then deal with it. If it is a problem with your delivery, use a reminder note at the next presentation.

Presentations for Upper Management

Presenting to upper management can be a killer. If you are seeking approval for a new networking plan from upper management, it is useful to know and comprehend their objectives. If they are currently worried that the company is old fashioned as to the use of Internet technology, you should emphasize the commercial aspects of the technology. Do not get into servers, clients, firewalls, etc. If they are concerned about their inabilities, you should emphasize ease of use with a very user-friendly interface.

It is difficult to overestimate the importance of careful preparation. Three minutes on the floor in front of upper management could decide the acceptance of a proposal of several months duration for you and your team. With so much potentially at stake, you must concentrate not only on the facts being presented, but also on the style, pace, tone, and ultimately the tactics that should be used. With upper management it is not a half-hour presentation you have to prepare for, but one of three minutes. You should focus, focus, and focus.

INTANGIBLES OF PRESENTATION SKILLS

In the end, it is not the techniques that are evaluated; it is how you handle the techniques that counts. There are a number of adjectives or phrases that are used, which are not measurable, that people will say about your presentation. The use of these intangibles means the result is the one measurable goal that you want, agreement to your idea. Some of these intangibles are as follows:

- Audience involvement or participation
- Captivating
- Effective
- Engaging
- Interesting
- Lively
- Logical

- Persuasive
- Powerful
- With confidence
- With poise

On the CD-ROM

1. 18Overview.ppt—Chapter Overview
2. 18Present.doc—Presentation Skills Self-Assessment

Section 6

Project Management Tools

This section describes four general project or operational management tools that can be used to support or enhance the skills discussed in the prior chapters. The four tools are time management, quality control management, risk management, and the use of three commonly available office application tools for handling projects or operational management situations.

In Chapter 19, you develop knowledge about the skills for using time management to achieve project goals in a timely manner.

In Chapter 20, you learn about the skills required to use quality control management to protect the integrity of project goals.

In Chapter 21, you learn about the skills used to have an effective and efficient risk management program.

In Chapter 22, you learn how to use three commonly available applications to assist in doing project management: Microsoft's Word 97, Excel 97, and PowerPoint 97.

Chapter 23 describes how to use the CD-ROM containing project management skills documentation (forms, checklists, and presentations) templates. All the self-assessments and checklists that relate to the information given in chapters throughout the book that are done in Microsoft Word 97 are presented here. The forms and presentations done in Microsoft Excel 97 and PowerPoint 97 are only listed.

CHAPTER 19

Time Management to Protect the End Date

Objectives: At the end of this chapter, you will be able to:

- Answer the question "What is time management?"

- Answer the question "What is a time estimate?"

- Answer the question "What is a schedule?"

- List five steps to develop a schedule.

- Identify four skills to handle an unrealistic schedule.

- Identify thirteen skills to manage a schedule.

- Identify three skills to handle schedule changes.

WHAT IS TIME MANAGEMENT?

Two important skills can make or break a project. The first skill is to establish correctly, objectively, and rationally the time estimates that are used to develop the project's schedule. The second skill is the proper handling of cost estimates used to develop the project's budget. Thus, a core skill of time management is managing time estimates. However, time management has two keystones. The other keystone is managing time for yourself. If you cannot use personal skills to manage your time, you cannot manage time for others and other project stakeholders will readily notice if you have this skill or not.

The skill to handle time estimates is the more important of the two skills. Time is a major factor in any cost estimate. You might say, "I am gong to buy a piece of equipment for $1000. Where is the need to determine time?" Are you going to use the equipment for 100 hours or a 1000 hours? You use the time factor for amortization.

Time management has at least three fundamental characteristics. The characteristics are as follows:

- Effectiveness—Producing the intent

- Efficiency—Producing maximum output with minimum input

- Effortlessness—Producing with ease

You have to make them apply to you and your daily routines as well as to the team and its day-to-day operations.

A formal definition of time management is a skill set that has to control a continuous project constraint that should be a consistent resource, that is time. Once it is gone, it cannot be replaced. First, it requires that you manage time so you do not have to answer yes to the following types of questions:

- Do I have problems allocating the team's work or my work to meet milestones?

- Do I let interruptions affect time for the team and myself?

- Does my communication system affect negatively the efficient use of project time?

- Do I lack the capability and the authority to say no to situations that affect time?

- Is overtime required to meet project goals?

Second, it requires that you not only ensure a "no" to the above questions, you also have to be a cop to time robbers. There are numerous time robbers, but many of them may reflect a lack of skills on your part. Ten ways you can control these robbers in a very personal manner are as follows:

- Be consistent in your decision making.

- Control telephone calls.

- Do not over-commit the team or yourself.

- Do your administrative duties correctly the first time.

- Ensure that you have an effective and efficient communication system.

- Ensure that you have the authority to get the job done.

- Do not disregard the corporate processes such as procurement.

- Do not have too many levels of review.

- Avoid having too many meetings.

- Say "no" when a request does not adhere to the measurable project goals.

One unique time robber for IT project managers is IT jargon. If people cannot comprehend what you say, they cannot meet or support your expectations.

WHAT IS A TIME ESTIMATE?

A time estimate should be an educated guess at the time parameters of an activity or a set of related activities. An IT project manager has an advantage over other project managers because of the availability of historical records on the system that can be used as benchmarks. When you finish your time estimates, you should have seven types of data:

- Criteria for associating cost and time estimates and potential changes

- Criteria for establishing time measurements

- Criteria for formulating time estimates

- Methodology for validating time estimates based on the defined project goals

- Procedure for associating time estimates with people, and equipment and people acquisition

- Quality control and validation time estimates (suggested 20 percent of your project)

- Time estimates based on skill types and levels rather than on headcount involved

NOTE:

The 20 percent for quality may seem high to you, but this does include time to minimize risk. This does not include time to resolve a major risk issue.

The closer you come to having the data as a part of the time estimates, the closer you come to managing the business managers' (strategic manager and people responsible for the budget) expectations. The estimates are concrete. A skill of time management is managing incorrect expectations.

What is a Schedule?

A schedule is a tool, not something that came off Mount Sinai. It is based on time estimates using experiences that in some cases may only be opinions. Scheduling is the process that formalizes the time estimates within a calendar structure. Unfortunately, the schedule and the budget are seen by business managers as written in concrete and can only be reduced.

The schedule is a document that links the sequences of activities, resource availability, start-end time dependencies, and lag-lead time relationships. The schedule is to time as the budget is to cost. A project schedule should be seen as written with a pencil—it can be erased as necessary.

It can be as elaborate as required to implement your project. It should be useable. An example of a schedule is a flow chart with milestones and times. There could also be links to essential players and groups and their responsibilities to the implementation of the project goals. A schedule should include the quality control milestones and the verification milestones.

One aspect of a schedule is the development of a critical path. One formal technique for scheduling is called *Critical Path Method* (CPM) which usually is used in conjunction with another scheduling tool, *Program Evaluation and Review Technique* (PERT). A highly simplified definition of a critical path is achieving the "must" requirements in a minimum of time. The critical path is the only part of the schedule that should be considered concrete. The critical path is the schedule in the truest sense that cannot be chipped at without approval by the customer.

FIVE STEPS TO DEVELOP A SCHEDULE

The first step in developing a schedule is for the team to estimate how much time each activity is worth and allocate only that amount. This critical appraisal may even suggest a different approach or method so that the time matches the task's importance. Beware of the desire for perfection. It takes too long. Time should be allocated for "fitness for a measurable goal," then stop. Your required skill is to keep the team on this path.

The second step of time management requires analyzing the milestone interrelationships. The sequence and duration (the time to accomplish the activity) of activities (primary and secondary) also need to be considered. The impact of resource requirements is equally important.

The third step is to have a schedule based on three levels of estimates. Any schedule is based on one of three levels of estimates, or a combination of two or all three. The levels of estimates are:

- Pessimistic—this position is that if something can go wrong, it will.

- Realistic—this position is there will be a few difficulties probably, but with compromise, difficulties will be overcome.

- Optimistic—this position is that everything will go as planned.

The reality of scheduling is that on some activities one position is taken, on some others another position is applied, and on what is left the third position is used. Even with the pessimistic position there are people who believe the project should go ahead even if they personally think the project is unrealistic. The one person who cannot have a completely pessimistic position is the project manager.

Fourth, to support a schedule, you need the following:

- Defined, measurable project goals

- Activities defined and ordered (put into a logical sequence)

- Activity costs

- Reliable time estimates

- Resources defined, including any special requirements and the time estimates for procuring them

- Essential time milestones defined

The schedule could be based on calendar time or on a critical path where the completion of a given event or set of events is important to the completion of the project goals.

The fifth step is to be sure you have access to the following ten data types when you develop a complete schedule:

- Change notification schedule

- Communications points scheduled

- Criteria for changing the schedule

- Critical path (optional)

- Quality control and validation schedule

- Schedule based on the scope definition

- Time allocated for risk management

- Time line (calendar, flow chart)

- Time line for acquiring skills, equipment, and materials

- Time lines that are consistent and coherent

FOUR SKILLS TO HANDLE AN UNREALISTIC SCHEDULE

If project planning and time management, especially the first draft of the schedule (an organizing and sequencing of time estimates) show that the project cannot be done, then time expectations are unrealistic. By knowing this at the project's potential start, you have a chance to do something about it.

An unrealistic deadline affects not only your success but also that of others. Suppose a product (a system enhancement) is scheduled for release too soon because you agree to deliver too early. Notice I did not say that the team agreed—the customer looks at you foremost for the validity of the schedule. A poorly defined schedule ripples rapidly into a tidal wave. Marketing and sales prepare customers to expect the product showing why they really need it. The product does not arrive on time. At a minimum the customers are dissatisfied. Even worse, customers are lost and the competition has advanced warning. This all happens because you do not have the skill set that challenges an unrealistic draft schedule.

You can avoid this situation. The project planning tells you how much time is realistically needed and the time management tells you how much time is available. This situation occurs only if your time estimates are based on objective benchmarks, are measurable, and are without padding. Padding is a hidden activity rather than an open activity to establish ranges of time (contingency planning).

There are at least four ways to deal with unrealistic deadlines:

- Obtain a deadline extension.

- Ask for more resources.

- Identify the priorities of the deliverable; perhaps only a part of the deliverable is necessary for the defined deadline.

- State the position clearly so that your strategic manager has fair warning, and assist in a schedule change with the customer.

If this method is not possible, consider the alternative. You need to consider moving to a company with realistic schedules.

THIRTEEN SKILLS TO MANAGE A SCHEDULE

The first step in managing a schedule is that you have to comprehend these ten points or "facts" about scheduling:

- A schedule is a plan to follow.

- Scheduling is a consequence of planning.

- Scheduling is an integration of sequencing activities, resource planning, cost estimating, and time estimating.

- Scheduling is at times more science than art.

- Scheduling is based on dependencies, the interrelationships of time, resources, and activities.

- Scheduling is concerned with the complete project.

- Scheduling is the automatic output from project management software.

- Scheduling may be thought of as a concrete process.

- A strategic manager looks at the schedule.

- The schedule is to time estimates as the budget is to cost estimates.

There is really only one principle an IT project manager must remember, which happens to be a principle of great IT management, "The scheduling output is only as reliable as the time estimating inputs."

The second step in managing a schedule is to use the above ten points as a basis for working with these interpersonal skills:

- Assert yourself on the requirement for a realistic schedule to achieve success.

- Communicate as necessary to achieve an effective and efficient schedule.

- Face a schedule crisis calmly; panic only makes the situation worse.

- Give and receive criticism on the status of the schedule when possible in private.

- Handle emotional stress of the customers, team members, and other project stakeholders using the schedule's rationality as a basis of discussion.

- Handle frustration and anger in the same manner you handle emotional stress.

- Handle time by saying no and by keeping a daily or weekly log of time management issues.

- Lead through example.

- Listen to the team's concern on time estimates and then the schedule.

- Respect other people's feelings on their time estimates and the impact the schedule has on their success.

- Relate to project stakeholders using the rationality that was used to develop the schedule.

- Sell your ideas to project stakeholders on necessary changes to the schedule.

- Take responsibility.

THREE SKILLS TO HANDLE SCHEDULE CHANGES

There are a number of interpersonal skills involved in change management for a schedule. There are however three techniques common to the management of schedule changes. The three techniques are as follows:

- Aligning the schedule

- Resolving slippage

- Correcting a schedule

Aligning the Schedule

One of the goals in time estimating was to get all the estimates before establishing the schedule. You did this and you have completed your schedule. There is one problem; the schedule says it will take six months longer to complete the project than the customer's requirement. If there is a lean schedule, here are six things you might do to realign the schedule:

- Define whether the date is absolute or flexible.

- Determine if the project can be done in segments.

- Diminish functionality.

- Increase resources (staff).

- Subcontract some of the functions.

- Waive office standards.

First work with the customer to see how concrete the end date is. If the customer is going to lose a large sum of money because of project failure then it is a no go. However, if there is slack time because of a general marketing effort, then a beginning effort can be made.

Second, check with the customer to see if the project can be done in segments. Determine how critical timing is in achieving the project goals.

Perhaps one goal can be completed the first quarter, another the second quarter, and then you can get back on a reduced schedule.

Third, consider reducing functionality. Perhaps one feature is critical, other features are needed over a broader period, and finally there may be one or more features that are just "desirable." Determine how the project can be realigned by this analysis.

Fourth, consider adding people. The customer needs to understand the effect on the price. You need to check on resources and working space availability. While in the planning stage it is easier to add staff than after the work begins.

Fifth, consider subcontracting some of the functionality. This is a variation on adding people, except you are going out of house to resolve the problem. You need to consider companies that specialize in the development required. They also may be able to do the development more quickly than in-house staff.

Sixth, consider—with higher management's approval—ignoring office rules as to when a person comes to work, or limiting paperwork requirements. A person may work better if they can come in midday and stay later rather than coming in at the standard hour.

If none of the six possibilities work to realign the schedule to the customer's satisfaction, there is one more option. The option is to just say no. The customer will consider that you have more integrity than if you attempt the schedule and fail. In addition, the customer may then reconsider the options.

Resolving Slippage

Some activity is going to come in late. What are you going to do about it? There are two types of slippages, the expected and the unexpected. The expected slippage you know about *before* the due date. The unexpected slippage is one that you learn about *after* the due date. One can manage the first, while the second is a no-no on the part of an operational manager.

The second should be prevented through open discussions at status meetings. This type of failure should be discussed in private with the offending manager. You need to be told why you were not informed. If a slippage happens very near the end of the activity it is one thing; however, if the slippage occurred early in the activity you might consider yourself misled. An unexpected slippage might be considered worse than being late. Not to be informed that a programmer who was expected to work on a project activity quit and a suitable replacement has not been found is a significant example of an unexpected slippage.

Here are some actions you can take to resolve a slippage:

1. Consider extension of the schedule.

2. Consider overtime as a last resort, because the budget quickly overruns.

3. Consider with the customer a reduction in the affected project goal; have supporting data.

4. Correct in private, but be firm.

5. Discover the extent of the slippage's impact; it may be minimal.

6. Do not panic.

7. Do not throw more resources into the pot to try to correct the slippage. There is always an activity learning curve.

8. Look for shortcuts or different approaches to accomplish the activity.

9. Use project management software to develop various scenarios for possible solutions.

Correcting a Schedule

You now have a schedule, but you think you might have errors. The following four-step approach can be used to assist you in making corrections:

- Analyze the schedule to identify any area that needs correction.

- Determine the course of action to make the correction.

- Revise the areas that require correction.

- Evaluate the new schedule for impacts.

Analysis could be handled in at least two ways. First, have the operational managers analyze their areas against the inputs. Second, use a time management tool to assist.

Course of action should be according to the type of errors found. The basic assumption is that you have time estimate errors rather than other types of errors.

In evaluating impacts, you need to consider duration, cost estimates, resource availability, lead-lag times, start-end dependencies, and potential slippage. The fifth step in this approach is to discuss the conclusions with the customer and get the customer's approval before finalizing the schedule to the team.

On the CD-ROM

1. 19Overview.ppt—Chapter Overview

2. 19TAsment1.doc—Time Management Self-Assessment

3. 19TAsment2.doc—Time Management Self-Assessment of Meeting Skills

CHAPTER 20

Quality Control Management Based on IT Standards

Objectives: At the end of this chapter, you will be able to:

- Answer the question, "What is quality control management?"
- Identify two basic components of the quality process.
- Develop a quality product that reflects ten characteristics.
- Identify twenty sources for errors in an IT project.
- Limit cost consequences.
- Ask three core questions about the quality control process.
- Ask ten basic questions about quality control.
- Identify the ten components of a quality assurance and control plan.
- Ask ten peer review questions.
- Determine the three configuration control functions.
- Identify five ISO quality process standards.
- Identify basic uses of statistics for quality management.
- Identify essential management involvement in quality control.

In this chapter, you learn about the skills required to use quality control management to protect the integrity of project goals. The foundation of quality control and assurance (the two components of the process) requires measurable objectives, standards, and benchmarks that can validate and establish variances of the working objectives. All else is commentary. The measurable objectives come from a statement of expectations from the customer and are technically clarified by the IT team. The benchmarks come from internal objective IT studies and from external standards from national and international IT organizations.

Quality is not Quality Circles, Just-in-Time, or Statistical Quality Control. Quality is an attitude that is a habit. All skills for managing quality support this principle: It takes longer to correct than it takes to do it correctly the first time.

NOTE:

Before reading this chapter, you should take the Quality Control Awareness Skills Self-Assessment found in Chapter 23 and on the CD-ROM (20QC.doc).

WHAT IS QUALITY CONTROL MANAGEMENT?

Quality control management is a process that consists of the two basic components of assurance and control. Quality as defined by those of the profession is "conformance to specification." Another way to state the purpose of the quality process is that it seeks to minimize performance errors.

Any skill set for managing quality has to be based on capabilities to interpret and enforce objective benchmarks and standards. While other functional managers may have to look outside of their groups for general benchmarks and standards, the IT manager does not. You only have to develop analyses of the daily output of network operational data. These data are location specific and usually have a high degree of consistency.

Assurance is based on performance. You need to establish performance standards and benchmarks, then measure and evaluate goal performance against these two things. Finally, assurance happens when you act on performance deviations. When someone says "assure" or "make sure" the objective is met, then you should be looking for the objective observable level of measurable success on the part of the developer(s), as well as product reliability.

Quality control happens when you act to meet the standards and benchmarks through the gathering of performance information, inspecting, monitoring, and testing. Control is the gathering, while assurance is the evaluating.

The essential word is "performance." This means you evaluate for quality accomplishment or achievement against:

- Corporate standards

- External benchmarks (vendor)

- External standards, such as ISO

- IT benchmarks (technical capabilities)

- IT budgetary goals

- IT standards

- Project measurable goals

- Project standards

- Schedule (structured time events)

Quality assurance and control can affect a number of areas including:

- Customer satisfaction (first and foremost)

- Design improvement

- Development enhancement

- Implementation integrity

- Testing certification

You have to use your management skill set so that quality assurance and control bring light to the darkest corner of any room in the IT house.

MANAGING SO QUALITY MEANS CUSTOMER SATISFACTION

Having a quality product can be summarized in two words, customer satisfaction. However you manage, you must ensure that your quality program has these ten characteristics that reflect customer satisfaction:

- Quality demonstrates an awareness of customer needs.
- Quality equates to control, a set of objective checks and balances.
- Quality is based on metrics so analysis can be done to determine degree of success.
- Quality is a commitment.
- Quality is measurable.
- Quality is support for the effort even when there are disagreements.
- Quality means avoidance of cost for things unnecessary.
- Quality means having the right skill at the right place and at the right time.
- Quality means there is communication between the customer and you.
- Quality revolves around coordination.

IT ERROR IDENTIFICATION

You can reduce the stress in an IT environment by having everyone put on their walls the list below. Every IT person has run into one or more of these errors. The question is, "How many have been caused by the IT person?" This list of twenty errors can easily be added to. The issue is why any of them have to happen in the first place.

1. Activity sequencing in error
2. Coding error

3. Database format error

4. Documentation error

5. Equipment is below standards

6. Failure to give timely reports

7. Feature not a part of a project goal

8. Hardware incompatibility

9. Material does not meet standards

10. Network component incompatibility

11. Not using appropriate standards

12. Operating system incompatibility to system infrastructure

13. Project activity not one defined in the schedule

14. Report layout in error

15. Requirement specification in error

16. Resource received is not in accordance with specification

17. Skill level is not valid

18. Software incompatibility

19. Training objectives do not meet a project goal

20. Vendor product incompatibility to system

Why do you want these errors eliminated? It improves customer satisfaction, read quality and more quality. Errors cost dollars, expensive dollars. You might eliminate some or even most of the errors without quality assurance and control; however, you will have no baseline to identify the extent of your accomplishment.

Cost Consequence Determinations

Remember consequence is defined as a negative impact on the work effort. You can use management software to assist you in determining cost consequences, but you can also use quality assurance and control to assist in this matter. The following are ten examples of cost consequences you should consistently analyze:

- Addition of staff, equipment, or materials
- Comparison of two or more vendor products
- Eliminating certain training components
- Eliminating certain types or components of user documentation
- Limiting or decreasing debugging time
- Limiting or decreasing testing time
- Decreasing potential maintenance time after product release
- Decreasing potential time for customer service
- Resolving an incompatibility problem
- Revising software or hardware requirements because of a revision of a project goal

Three Core Questions about Your Quality Control Process

The following are three questions you need to answer so the dark things in the night do not attack you.

- Do you have a consistent set of quality standards?
- Do you have a quality control system that has assurance and control?
- Have you established validation activities?

The forefront of defining IT activities should be quality control. Do you know of a project that was completed without a change? You must have activities that show how you handle change. This point is not negotiable because you need consistency to have quality assurance and control.

It is recommended to have at least two lines in your budget for quality control management. The lines are assurance and control. You may want to divide these two lines into salaries, equipment, and materials. A quarterly budget reduction of a one-line item can produce a consequence similar to a dark thing in the night.

QUESTIONS TO ASK FOR A QUALITY ASSURANCE AND CONTROL PROCESS

Perhaps the first skill in developing a quality program is simply asking a set of questions to determine its status or direction. The responses to the questions have to reflect that quality is not only impacted by what happens within the IT group, but also in other functional groups such as training and documentation.

Has a comprehensive quality control program been defined including standards and benchmarks? The basis for defining the quality control process is through related standards and benchmarks. There need to be specified quality control points throughout the entire project process. The quality control process should be defined separately from the testing process and more as the validating one.

Has the quality management process been cost estimated and budgeted? It is recommended that you have at least two budget lines for quality: control and assurance. Do not hide quality expenses in other budgetary lines.

Have the quality control events been included at appropriate milestones in operational activities (service) and IT projects? The quality control and verification milestones should be clearly defined within any schedule. The quality control management timeline may be defined as a separate timeline, however, when and where quality control and assurance flows into the main part of a project or a key set of operational activities must be stated.

What is the necessary time for quality validation? Quality control activities need to be established throughout a schedule. Never schedule all of the quality assurance for the end or last phase of a project.

What are the criteria for documenting quality control activities? Some people think the writing group does all documentation, which is far from the truth. There need to be criteria or standards for IT design and development documentation. These types of documentation are the foundation for the customer documentation developed by the writing group. You have to establish documentation requirements and have to identify who is responsible for writing and editing each document.

What are the quality control procedures that need to be in the activity plan? There should be quality control procedures to cover all activities, not just the results of operational activities. The quality control team can be used as an objective benchmark for viewing operational or project status as long as they do not become bogged down in red tape.

What are the quality control procedures that ensure correct sequencing? Quality control considerations are universal to all activities. You need to establish quality control activities linked into all sequences. There need to be validation points throughout a set of operational activities or a project.

What are the standards and benchmarks for quality control? As used here, a standard is usually an external, industry-accepted procedural document for achieving quality for any IT defined goals. Benchmarks are specific technical levels of excellence. These standards and benchmarks should be collected and placed in a location available to any IT member.

What is the impact of the quality control and assurance processes on time estimates? Quality control should have a specific amount of time allocated. You could set a benchmark of say twenty percent. This percentage is of the estimated time for a project or your estimated annual workload.

What quality control policies, benchmarks, or standards have to be followed? Has it been determined what the impact is of outside policies such as federal rules or standards, on IT? Any large or even a small company may have three different procedures for contracting outside people, for leasing equipment, and for buying materials. You need to be prepared for the various procedures from different functional groups that might affect your IT operations.

BASIC REQUIREMENTS FOR A QUALITY PLAN

You need a quality plan that defines the role of quality control in all phases of a project and one that covers day-to-day operational activities. It includes definitions for deliverables, functions, and specific activities required of quality control and assurance to ensure successful completion of all activities. Quality procedures that are specific to a project should also be identified in an appendix of a project or operational plan document.

You need a set of quality metrics that defines how the introduction and maintenance of a new networking (Internet or intranet) enhancement or application is measured, attained, and controlled. A project plan should include special quality procedures and references to existing operational procedures.

The quality plan should summarize the staff, resources, and equipment required by quality assurance and control to perform specific activities and to support a new application. Notes on where the funds are located for these items would be most helpful.

The quality plan should be updated before each major phase review for a project or on a quarterly basis for operational activities to reflect changes. A quality plan that is not reviewed on a regular basis is not a quality plan.

MANAGING PEER REVIEWS

A peer review is a technical meeting called for one purpose, to review a deliverable. There has to be a final review of the complete set of deliverables; however, there should also be a series of peer reviews for each significant deliverable.

> **NOTE:**
>
> Management, this includes the project manager, should be absent, so the technical review does not turn into individual performance reviews.

You need to have a training program so people can handle a peer review correctly. People should not go into a design document review and be concerned about commas and periods. The peer review is the place to ask a number of hard technical questions. Depending on the type of deliverable, the following questions might be asked:

- Does documentation correctly state technical requirements?
- Does it meet appropriate standards?
- Does it meet corporate benchmarks?
- Does it meet functional requirements?
- Does it meet operational requirements?
- Does it meet protocol requirements?
- Does it meet security requirements?
- Does it technically fulfill project goals?
- Does the help function assist the customer in resolving technical issues?
- Have training courses been developed to cover technical issues correctly?

Peer reviews need their appropriate allocations for time in a schedule. There are many types of peer reviews, including:

- Capacity plans
- Coding
- Documentation
- Implementation plan
- Internetworking plan
- Project plan
- System design
- System development
- Test plan
- Training plan
- "X" technical plan (example, vendor technical specification)

Each peer review has its own deliverable. This deliverable should be treated with the importance that is its due. The deliverable could impact either schedule or the budget or both, which is usually the case. Specific technical statements should be made about the deliverable.

One method for developing better peer reviews is to have regular weekly meetings (too much? Well, try monthly) to discuss quality. This strategy requires care. The benefit is that regularity might lead to habit. The formal opportunity permits the expression of ideas and the inclusion of the group. You are looking for an emphasis on collective responsibility. The objective of regular meetings is to establish a foundation for accepted behavior toward quality.

Management of Configuration Control

Configuration control is important to everyone, whether it be hardware or software. *Everyone* here means also the customer. When the customer says the product is too hard to use, they usually mean there is a configuration problem. *Configuration* as used here means issues involving the correct version, not the values or parameters used to make a product work correctly.

At the project level, the team relies on deliverables from each other. When a team member works for a time on a deliverable and then finds out it is an incorrect version and the work has to be redone, is there frustration and stress? To eliminate this frustration and stress, a project should have a process, method, or mechanism that does the following:

- Identifies deliverable versions

- Describes differences between or among versions

- Ensures that any team member can get the most recent version

When you have a mechanism with the above three functions, you have a management and control tool. It is essential to have all three. The version should be marked on the outside of the product packaging or documentation so the team member can instantly determine version level.

Quality and the ISO

The view of quality is becoming international. One of the most critical areas for international standards is in the informational system and technology environment. You need to know about the functions and goals of the International Organization for Standardization (ISO) which is a consortium that sets standards in a variety of areas. The following five ISO standards are important to quality:

- *ISO 9000* is a quality system standard for any product, service, or process.

- *ISO 9001* is a quality system standard for design, production, and installation of a product or service.

- *ISO 9002* is a quality system model for quality assurance in production and installation.

- *ISO 9003* is a quality system model for quality assurance in final inspection and testing.

- *ISO 9004* is a set of quality management guidelines for any organization to use to develop and implement a quality system.

Because of the importance of these standards in the business world, especially for businesses involved in international activities, you should become aware of the ISO if you are not already. These standards are not just for an IT organization but for a corporation or a division that is responsible for a complete product.

USE OF STATISTICS FOR QUALITY

You can easily lie with statistics, but statistics can also assist you in seeing the truth better. If you cannot measure an improvement, then there is no improvement.

Gathering statistics has at least five benefits:

- Identifies a problem's parameters

- Allows for the monitoring of progress

- Provides an objective criterion for continuing with an idea

- Justifies expenses based on observed improvements

- Displays achievement

Statistics must be gathered in an objective and empirical manner. The result should be displayed as simply as possible. You might want to monitor the number of bugs discovered. You could have a chart with the number of bugs rather than listing them all.

In the long term, you might automatically gather statistics on a wide range of issues such as complaints, bug reports, machine downtime, etc.

These statistics can provide early warning of unexpected problems or comparative data. The statistics need to focus on product performance, not on individual performance.

MANAGEMENT INVOLVEMENT

There is one fixed rule for all managers involved in an IT project or day-to-day operations: Do not let quality slide when deadlines are too, too close for comfort. To do this will take you out of the frying pan and put you in the fire.

Quality requires a long-term view of success, not a short-term gain. Quality can be seen as a nebulous activity until near the end of a project or a year-end review of operational activities. Each manager must recognize that the results of quality for a project can result in an improved view by the customer as to the corporation's integrity and thus improve the bottom line. Quality lessens the need for customer service; that is, the type of service that has to resolve product bugs in the field.

In summary, you need to do the following:

- Place quality planning at the top of your agenda.
- Be sure there are significant time and cost estimates for:
  — Monitoring activities
  — Testing deliverables
  — Evaluating performance
  — Measuring performance
  — Correcting performance deviations, errors
- Guarantee there are time estimates for peer reviews.
- Have a configuration control mechanism.
- Create an appropriate reporting system on quality issues.

- Assure that quality issues stay at the deliverable level rather than being considered personal.

- Have separate lines in the budget for quality assurance and control.

- Have a location where all standards and any other quality-related documentation is available to all.

ON THE CD-ROM

1. 20Overview.ppt—Chapter Overview
2. 20QC.doc—Quality Control Awareness Skills Self-Assessment
3. 20QCQts—Quality Control and Deliverables Questions

CHAPTER 21

Risk Management to Identify the Holes

Objectives: At the end of this chapter, you will be able to:

- Answer the question, "What is a risk?"

- Answer the question, "What is risk management?"

- Answer the question, "What is risk analysis?"

- Identify types of sources that can cause risks.

- Explain the impacts of different categories of risks.

- Ask questions on the risk management process.

- Establish the criteria for a risk that may impact your activities.

- Develop documentation requirements and standards for risk management.

- Explain how risk and opportunity are two faces of the same coin.

- Create risk management documents.

- Identify essential management involvement in risk management.

In this chapter, you learn about the skills used to have an effective and efficient risk-management program. Two skill sets you need are skills to identify risks and skills to manage risks.

> **NOTE:**
>
> Before reading the chapter, you should take the Risk Management Skills Self-Assessment. It is found in Chapter 23 and on the CD-ROM (21Risk.doc).

WHAT IS A RISK?

A risk is not just any problem, bug, or variance. A risk is a performance error that can have a significant or disastrous impact on your success.

WHAT IS RISK MANAGEMENT?

Risk management involves three functions:

- Identify the risk.
- Assess the risk.
- Allocate resources to resolve the risk.

Risk management is the skill set required to resolve both negative and positive opportunities. The emphasis is usually only on the negative. Risk management was developed as a tool to minimize liabilities. A *risk* (one of those monsters in the darkest part of the closet) is a problem that will adversely affect the IT group. An *opportunity* is a situation that will positively affect the project in time, money, resources or all three in a significant manner.

Risk management is a generic management tool in that there are no special tool definitions for this activity. It is applicable all the time. Risk management begins when you walk through the door to be an IT manager. My first call, and in the first hour of being on the job as a senior manager, was a defining moment in risk management to say the least. An employee had made a major financial and resource commitment without discussion with the prior manager.

For a project, risk management could begin as early as a customer coming to you to discuss an idea for a project. Notice the word "idea." The customer may think there is a project. You need to ask the customer a minimum of three questions:

1. Is there money in the customer's budget for the project?

2. Has the customer formed a project definition and appropriate milestones?

3. Does support exist by all affected parties for the project?

A "no" to any of these questions is a flag that there is a risk. The project is an *idea*. Risk management in this case is asking the correct questions to ensure there is a potential project, not just an idea.

> **NOTE:**
>
> To further eliminate risk with the above mythical customer, you should try to get a set of measurable objectives from the customer. It should be more than "I need a firewall." You must find out what the customer's specific expectations are. You should fill in the technical requirements.

WHAT IS RISK ANALYSIS?

Risk analysis is a technique, tool, or method for assessing either quantitatively or qualitatively (or both) the impacts of an identified risk or a potential risk uncovered through a scenario. Risk management is the course of action you use to solve the risk.

When you use risk analysis you are comparing alternatives to determine tradeoffs for actions, durations, resources, and skills. Risk analysis should be an objective tool that defines the technical parameters of a risk. The harder part is determining the emotional parameters.

The comparison might come in three flavors: best, worst, or viable. This concept is the basis of Program Evaluation and Review Technique (PERT). We all have a rational criterion for risk analysis in the work environment: if worse than fifty percent, forget it. There are many exceptions to this criterion, such as start-up companies and one's personal life (betting on winning the lottery).

One can approach risk analysis from many different viewpoints. Any approach might include these core steps:

- Develop a model.

- Identify unknown qualities or quantities.

- Analyze the model through scenarios or simulations.

- Decide on a solution.

There is one risk one might never think of, but all project managers experience it. It is the risk that business managers think that when you do risk analysis you are an alarmist. Business managers tend to consider risks serious only when they happen. You overcome this by:

- Documenting all risks

- Keeping management informed

- Presenting measurable recommendations

- Making sure management comprehends the consequences

- Keeping a neutral position by never saying, "I told you so."

RISK SOURCE IDENTIFICATION

A risk could have a disastrous effect on any IT activity, especially one built on sand. Some of the sources of risk include:

1. Activity sequencing in error

2. Coding error

3. Database format error

4. Documentation error

5. Equipment is below standards

6. Failure to give timely reports

7. Feature not a part of a project goal

8. Hardware incompatibility

9. Material does not meet standards

10. Network component incompatibility

11. Not using appropriate standards

12. Operating system incompatibility to system infrastructure

13. Project activity not one defined in the schedule

14. Report layout in error

15. Requirement specification in error

16. Resource received is not in accordance with specification

17. Skill level is not valid

18. Software incompatibility

19. Training objectives do not meet a project goal

20. Vendor product incompatibility to system

The goal of risk management should be to share the risk impacts when possible in an equitable manner. There should not be a "dumping on" one party unless it is clearly shown that the party is the only party causing the risk. The reality is that this situation is probably ludicrous.

> **NOTE:**
>
> Usually an electronic risk analysis tool focuses on the threat mode. However, through a reverse of variables one can develop scenarios for opportunities. If the customer decides that you have an extra six months to complete the project, you can input this variable into a risk-analysis model and look for opportunities. In this case, one might also find risks because of the unavailability of resources beyond the original finish date.

RISK SOURCE DETERMINATION

Risks come in all colors and shapes. There are at least eight common sources of risks for day-to-day IT operations and projects. Here is a short list of sources for risks:

- Customer
  - Financial support becomes unavailable
  - Not participating in agreed upon reviews
  - Response time to questions is not timely
  - Seems to have new interpretations of goals
  - Skill resources availability degrades
- Delivery
  - Product does not meet functional requirements according to standards

- — Product has incompatibility issues
- — Product has interoperability issues
- — Product's capacity exceeds available capacity
- — Product's response time is inadequate
- Equipment
  - — Does not meet specifications
  - — Limited availability
  - — Missed delivery date
- People
  - — Lacking in skills required
  - — Not available at time required
  - — Not available because of job change
- Physical
  - — Critical computers or hardware fail
  - — Data stolen
  - — Facility lost through fire or another catastrophe
  - — Virus infects some critical data
- Goals
  - — Customer identifies the need for additional effort
  - — New requirements are identified
  - — An operational manager makes a change without approval
- Technology
  - — Technical assumptions are not factual
  - — Technical constraints cannot be overcome
  - — Technology is not understood clearly
  - — Technology is too new

- Vendor

  — Financial failure

  — Not participating in agreed upon reviews

  — Response to questions is not timely

  — Seems to have new interpretations of goals

  — Skill resources availability degrades

What is your opinion of your skill set for managing risks at this point? You slowly go through the above list and think through how you would manage each of these situations. Do not wait until one of them happens to you.

ASK THE IMPORTANT QUESTIONS FOR RISK MANAGEMENT

To establish a risk management process you need to ask yourself two core questions and consider some basic principles for managing the risk management process. The two questions are the following:

1. Do you have a list of constraints (guidelines) and assumptions for handling potential threats and opportunities?

2. Are there identified fixed points in the project cycle or in day-to-day operations for assessing risks?

There should be defined activities for handling threats. You should also have activities that handle opportunities if they arise. A simple activity rule would be: "Until a threat (an opportunity) reaches a certain threshold (your definition) no action shall be taken."

Risk assessment is important to planning resources. You need to determine what are the minimum skill-level requirements. Notice a headcount requirement is *not* used. Perhaps for some activities a novice can do them, while for other activities an expert is needed. Remember a lack of a skill can be turned into an opportunity.

In your budget, there should be a separate item for risk management. The most logical line is the one to allocate money for contractors. Another line to consider if one is established is for quality control and verification. Your product may need more testing than you estimated.

ASKING BASIC QUESTIONS ON RISK MANAGEMENT

The following questions are asked in the context of a project, but are valid for day-to-day IT operations. The word "team" can easily be replaced with "IT group." Risk knows no language boundaries. The customer's needs are paramount. The stopping of the cracker is paramount.

What are the criteria for risk management that may impact activities? The first set of criteria is not necessarily based on sophisticated risk analysis but on the experiences of the team (IT group). If the team lacks in experience, perhaps it is advisable for an outside expert to give advice on these criteria.

Are there any training requirements for risk management? One should not necessarily expect the quality team to be trained already to assess and monitor a new product and in particular to do risk assessments and evaluations. They may have to go to a class on protocols or learn a new standard related to the product. They may be experts on the quality process, but not technically knowledgeable about the assumptions and constraints of the product to be developed.

Does the project schedule have appropriate links from the quality control schedule to all other areas of the schedule? A performance error can happen anywhere in the project process. The quality assurance and control group needs to evaluate and assess the error's potential as a risk. Because of these two requirements, quality needs to have links into all project activities.

What are the direct-cost estimates for risk management activities? There is the managing of risks *after* they are identified, and managing them *before* they happen, to minimize risks. Direct-cost estimates should be for risk prevention. This is for the risk-management structure and ongoing process. There should also be contingency funds for resolving risks. This amount is determined by the significance of the project's results. While risk management is the responsibility of everyone, you may wish to associate your risk-management responsibilities with the quality group.

What are the documentation requirements and standards for risk management? You need to establish in the planning phase criteria for when a performance error becomes a risk. Risk criteria should be established against the project goals and against appropriate standards. You should have a risk form that should be available to everyone to be used in a risk analysis and evaluation. This is so everyone can expect the types of information to be gathered for risk management. Finally, but not the least, any IT risk management policies and procedures should be fully utilized in the project.

What are the essential project activities managing risks? If you identify risk management as an associated responsibility of quality assurance and control then the general activities may seem straightforward. There may also be special risk-management tasks generated because of the project goals and the failure to achieve any one of them. Ultimate responsibility for risk management resides in the hands of the project manager.

What are the resources required for risk management? Resource requirements should be an extension of the resources for quality assurance and control. There may be special equipment required to handle risk potential based on the project goals.

What are the skills and their levels required for risk management? The project goals should assist in developing the skill definitions. There are the technical skills to resolve certain types of risks; however, there may be other types of skills also required. Early in the planning phase, there should be a list drawn up of potential risks by the project team. This list should focus on the technical risks rather than other areas. This list could be used to identify the other required skills.

What are the time estimates for risk management? There should be some slack time allocated for major groups of activities to resolve minimal risks. A large risk requires a complete evaluation of the project's status. Time is then defined in how long it takes you to control a disaster.

What procedures, standards, or policies govern risk management? The first standards that should be brought to the table are those IT standards involving risks. Other standards are those that assist in defining the project goals. Project risk management should be consistent with any corporate policies, procedures, or standards for risk management.

RISK AND OPPORTUNITY AS TWINS

Most people think of risks only as a threat to the goals. What if you find a new product that can ease your project goals by tenfold? Let us do some dreaming. Is this a risk? It is similar to finding out the configuration for a product is going to take twice as long. You say no. Have you considered the implication of the new product on your whole project? Do you have to set new expectations? Do you now have the opportunity (read as *requirement*) to add additional functionality and services to your project?

RISKS AND OPPORTUNITIES DOCUMENTATION

Because risks come in two forms, threats and opportunities, both should be equally documented. Given here are examples of two important risk management documents:

- Business Justification
- Risk Assessment

Business Justification

The Business Justification shows how the achieved goals of the project will improve your company's bottom line and make more effective financial relationships with another company or with your venders or customers. In this light, doing a business justification and sharing it with others is necessary perhaps for your survival or at least your good health. The Business Justification assures that the current view of the project performance meets previous commitments and management expectations. The document may have a one or more year(s) view of:

- Revenues

- Maintenance Costs

- Investment

- Return on Investment (ROI)

- Customer Impact

NOTE:

A Business Justification could be used, and is probably used, to explain for the annual budget any significant day-to-day operational services such as general networking maintenance. In some rare cases, you may have to make a business justification for customer service.

Risk Assessment

It is important that any risk assessment consider both threats and opportunities. All involved parties should review the Risk Assessment document. When there are too many people to do the review, there should at least be representatives from each component. Perhaps only one or two important vendors should do the review for all the others. A risk assessment should be done at least at every major project phase. You also need to consider quarterly risk assessments for day-to-day operations.

The Risk Assessment should be against established thresholds. An example of a threshold is that no action is taken until a certain number of errors are found over a given period.

MANAGEMENT INVOLVEMENT

Each manager must recognize that the results of delivering a quality product with minimal performance errors can be an improved view by the customer as to the corporation's integrity and thus can improve the bottom line. As mentioned in Chapter 20, a quality product lessens the need for customer service to resolve product bugs in the field. There needs to be a commitment from all of the managers to analyze and evaluate identified risks quickly and with integrity. Resolve the risk rather than spending time to search for someone to blame.

RISK MANAGEMENT SCENARIO: INSTALLING A FIREWALL

This a template for thinking about the risks involved in the installation of a firewall into your IT network. This details how to minimize not only the risks, but also the potential portals to disaster.

First, you need to be aware of the potential types and levels of security risks that may already be present in your system before you identify your requirements. Second, you need to know what would be the role of a firewall in your IT network. A broad formal definition of a firewall is it is used to guard your private network, intranet, from the public network, the Internet. About all you get from this definition is that it is a guardian between two types of networks. What you really need is to acquire from a variety of firewall vendors their specifications and do an analysis to consider what these firewalls have in common, and then their differences. You then compare this analysis against your list of potential risks.

You need to also know what types of risks a firewall cannot mitigate. There are "backdoor" types of risks such as worms in e-mail attachments. There is also the disgruntled employee.

One concern of identifying the security level is the level of integration of your intranet with the Internet. There is a different level of security between just using an Internet service such as e-mail and having a Web-based intranet.

Another concern is determining the types of data that require protection. The position that all data must be protected at the same level is unrealistic. You may consider "moats" of firewalls around certain strategic data that if lost could cause a major crisis for the company. You do not need necessarily to protect training and customer documentation files, but financial data and marketing strategies need to be protected.

A consideration of the type of firewall required is to compare the importance of data against the likelihood of attack. There is a belief that most attacks are never noticed.

The following is a short list of other types of security concerns:

- Financial status

- Motivation of attacker

- Reputation of company

- Safety

- Type of attacker (youth versus spy)

A common question when the issue of risk management arises is "Should we have a formal risk assessment?" A security professional probably would say yes; however, it is most likely that your IT group has been concerned with risks from day one and managing risks has become a part of the day-to-day operations. Risk management should be ingrained in IT policies and procedures. Such issues may arise when the IT project is for another corporate organization.

There are three ways to do security analysis:

- Tiger team
- Brainstorming
- Security engineering procedures

The first is usually used when you have an established security system and you have a known security breach. This method would not be used during project planning. However, designated members of a tiger team could be involved in the second method, brainstorming. The early stage of project planning usually takes on the characteristics of structured brainstorming. The third method should be integrated into the activities of the project risk-management team.

For the integration of a firewall into your IT network you have to do all the project functions. The project context is the defined expectations of the firewall to protect the selected data and to provide the level of security needed. You have to

- Define activities.
- Sequence the activities.
- Do cost, time, and resource estimates.
- Do a schedule.
- Do a budget.
- Manage and control the project events.

SURVEYS AND CHECKLISTS FOR CREATING A RISK-ANALYSIS MODEL

For a risk-analysis model to have validity, you must have adequate input, step one of the process. One way to develop input is to create either a survey or a checklist for determining how to establish the input. Any survey or checklist must consider four areas:

- Activity sequences

- Duration of activities

- Resource availability

- Spending and revenue expectations

The following is a set of twenty survey questions that might assist you in the creation of a risk-analysis model:

1. Have all operational activity sequences been identified?

2. Have all training activity sequences been identified?

3. Have all milestones been identified?

4. Have all documentation activity sequences been identified?

5. Have all quality control points been identified?

6. Are there standards or benchmarks for comparing activity durations?

7. Have operational cost estimates been identified?

8. Have indirect cost estimates been identified?

9. Have all revenue dates been identified?

10. Have available skills been identified?

11. Have deliverable dates been identified?

12. Have status report dates been identified?

13. Has a critical path been established?

14. Have critical equipment requirement dates been established?

15. Have critical material requirement dates been established?

16. Are there "slippage" dates?

17. Have software infrastructure benchmarks (configuration, compatibility, and so forth) been identified?

18. Have hardware infrastructure benchmarks (interoperability, portability, and so forth) been identified?

19. Have the dates, equipment, and resources been entered from all vendors and consultants?

20. Have skill level benchmarks been identified?

The following is a checklist that is similar to the survey above. The survey does not require answers beyond yes or no, even when it is possible to elaborate. In addition, the checklist requires more detail than the survey. The underlying question of a checklist is "Have you considered this item?" This checklist is for the core hardware infrastructure of an IT network.

Hosts

Mainframe

Server (each of your server types should be listed)

CPUs

Mainframes

Operating systems (each type should be listed)

Intermediate Nodes

Bridges

Firewalls

Gateways

Hubs

Routers

Switches

Terminals (all appropriate types should be noted)

Workstations (all appropriate types should be noted)

Peripheral Nodes

Faxes

Printers

Applications

Operations (all appropriate ones should be noted)

User (all appropriate ones should be noted)

Code

Executable (identify areas of impact)

Source (identify areas of impact)

Databases

Buffer size

Cache

Number of users (users impacted by project)

Disk

Cache

Controller speed

Drivers

Load balance

GUI Components

Servers

System

Memory Components

Cache type

Size

Speed

Protocols

Intranet

Internet

System

Server Protocols

Chat

Directory

E-mail

File

News

Search

IT Tools

Blueprints

Equipment diagrams

Inventories

Management

Performance analyzers

Policies

Process flowcharts

Protocol analyzers

Wiring route map

This detailed checklist was given here for a number of reasons. First, one needs to comprehend the level of detail required to do adequate risk analysis. Second, while many of these may not be required for a given project, they should be considered for any project. If you do not have adequate equipment diagrams for a project that has important IT network hardware enhancements you might have a potential risk. Third, this is a template for other checklists for budget definitions, skill definitions, and so forth.

ON THE CD-ROM

1. 21Overview.ppt—Chapter Overview

2. 21Risk.doc—Risk Management Skills Self-Assessment

3. 21RiskQts.doc—Risk Analysis Activity Questions

4. 21RAMSurvey.doc—Survey Questions for Creating a Risk Analysis Model

CHAPTER 22

Non-IT Computerized Management Tools

Objectives: At the end of this chapter, you will be able to:

- Use common tools versus using special management tools.
- Use Microsoft Excel to enhance IS basic management skills.
- Use Microsoft PowerPoint to enhance IS basic management skills.
- Use Microsoft Word to enhance IS basic management skills.
- Identify dangers when using general software applications.

In this chapter, you will learn how to use three commonly available office applications to assist in doing management: Microsoft Word, Microsoft Excel, and Microsoft PowerPoint. It is these common tools that we tend to forget to use as management tools. One thinks usually only of these tools for documents, financial spreadsheets, and data presentations.

> **NOTE:**
>
> Data presentation is used here instead of informational presentation because most people think data and information are the same. Information is the integration of a set of data so that a common conclusion can be reached by all readers or viewers. The presentation of information is a management skill. For more details on presentation skills see Chapter 18.

While Microsoft's Excel, PowerPoint, and Word are the focus of the chapter, the principles given are the same for any spreadsheet, graphics package, or word processor. The use of these Microsoft applications can make your work easier because of their compatibility, interoperability, and portability.

The use of any IT management tool for networking is usually based on special vendor information and how your informational system is configured. These highly specialized tools should be used for developing objective benchmarks. These tools are especially important in managing quality control and risk issues.

NOTE:

Before reading the chapter, you should take three self-assessments on these office applications. They are found in Chapter 23 and on the CD-ROM (22Word.doc, 22PPT.doc, and 22Excel.doc).

USE OF A PROFESSIONAL MANAGEMENT TOOL

This section looks at reasons you might desire to use common tools or applications for managing rather than a complex tool. The principle applicable here is true in the selection of any application: The more bells and whistles it has; the less user-friendly it is. In addition, the learning curve for more complex tools is extremely sharp. This is not to say that to use any of the applications discussed in the chapter does not require a learning curve. Most users probably use significantly less than twenty percent of any given application's functions. For the word processor, you commonly use only the given font type and size, page format, save, and print.

> **NOTE:**
>
> I have seen e-mails from authors of books on computers who do not know how to set up headers and footers using Word.

Four general areas where software may assist you are:

- Activity sequences
- Time estimates
- Cost estimates
- Resource definitions

No amount of software can be better than the user's skill set. Below are ten specific examples of project management requirements where software might assist in the analysis of the many variables of a project (for example, the four areas above produce ten pairs of variables):

- Cost analysis with variances
- Critical paths
- Data summaries
- Forecasting
- Graphic reports
- Reports
- Resource planning
- Risk analysis
- Scenarios ("what if")
- Time analysis with variances

With any special management tool or a set of administrative applications, you might use them to do:

- Analyzing

- Monitoring

- Planning

- Predicting

- Reporting

- Scheduling

- Tracking

From the above two lists, the software features and functions you need to consider in the use of software include:

- Control mechanism for time, costs, and resources

- Cost effectiveness through either purchase or lease

- Dates, calendar, and schedule

- Graphic display such as the Gantt chart

- Memory requirements minimum for maximum efficiency

- Networking schema

- Report generator

- Sort capability

- System capacity adequate for a number of project activities

- Update capability

As an IT manager you may be more fortunate than most functional managers in that you may have someone on your technical staff who has used a specialized management tool. Actually, the only places where you might find users are in the marketing or training groups. The point here is that you as the IT manager should just "bite the bullet" and learn how to use a complex management tool. Until you have the time, you can use effectively and efficiently some of the common applications available.

> **NOTE:**
> ——————
>
> Novice users tend to generate reports that are so hard to read or too time consuming to read that any effectiveness in the use of a specialized management tool is completely lost.

USE OF EXCEL TO MANAGE

In this section we look at some very simple examples of using Excel to assist you in managing and controlling a project for the core areas:

- Project activity sequences (database)
- Time (Gantt chart)
- Resources (database)
- Costs (spending analysis)

Constructing an Activity Sequence Database

Prior to using a project management tool such as Microsoft's Project Manager or IMSI's TurboProject, you need to have a precise sense of all your activity and pertinent data such as:

- Measurable name ("write code" is too general, "code for a specific function or feature" is somewhat better).
- Operational group code (P for programming, D for documentation, T for Training, PT for programming test, and so forth).

- Priority level (assists in developing a critical path, either 1, 2, and 3, or H, M, and L)

- Start date

- End date

- Work requirement (hours or days)

- Cost estimate

- Special hardware requirement (Y or N)

- Documentation requirement (Y or N)

- Training requirement (Y or N)

- Optional notes (any special consideration)

The steps for constructing this database are as follows:

1. On the first row label the columns with data from above such as task, group, priority, and so forth.

2. Beginning with the second row, enter the data as you receive it; you may do sorting later.

3. At any time you can highlight *all* the cells with data and do a sort.

   — Click on data on the Menu bar.

   — Click Sort.

   — Select your sort options, up to three columns either ascending or descending order.

   — Click on OK.

4. If you want to keep this sorted worksheet, do a File ➜ Save As with a new file name.

There are many things you can determine from this basic database. Here are five of the sort possibilities:

- *Group and start date* give you task order by group.

- *Start date* gives you all tasks in order.

- *Work requirements* can give you shortest task to longest task or in reverse.

- *Cost estimates* can give you from the least amount to the largest amount or in reverse.

- You can do sorts so you identify readily all tasks that have special requirements such as hardware, documentation, and training.

You might also total the work requirement and cost estimates column, then in the cell one down divide this total by number of tasks to get an average. After a sort, you can find the median value for either of these columns.

Because you have readily available start and end dates you can easily produce a Gantt chart. This type of database makes it easy for your managers to verify their data.

You must have an agreement from all users for a template and input, and then have each user construct an individual worksheet. At this point, you can then merge all the worksheets as one.

NOTE:

For day-to-day IT operational use, instead of using *P* for *programming*, you would incorporate IDs for each group or functional unit. This technique could be used to develop the annual IT budget. The managing of an IT organization on an annual basis is similar to managing a very complex project that lasts a year. The two management situations are similar, but not the same. Just one significant distinction is management's attitudes toward the function of the budget. One's interpersonal skill set is different in this case.

Constructing a Simple Gantt Chart

A Gantt chart is a technique for presenting timelines in a horizontal bar mode. The first column is for tasks, while the other columns are for dates. This technique has been around for a hundred years. The basic characteristics are activities listed by priority and sequence with start- and end-dates, and bars in two contrasting colors to represent activity completion. Additional characteristics include:

- Legend

- Milestone symbols

- Overdue indicators

- Notes (outside of the chart)

There are nine steps in constructing a simple Gantt chart in an Excel worksheet:

1. Starting with the second column, place the project timeline across the first row (days, weeks, and so forth).

2. Beginning with the second row, place the tasks (major tasks could be made bold and sub-tasks normal).

3. Using the color option, format the rows to represent the durations of tasks in a dark color (update using a light color).

4. Select the cell or cells you want to format.

5. Click *Format* on the Menu bar.

6. Click on *Cells.*

7. Click on *Patterns.*

8. Under *Cell Shading Color,* click colored box of preference.

9. Click on *OK.*

> **NOTE:**
>
> The use of red and green as contrasting colors is not recommended because they carry a high emotional significance. In addition, yellow is a color that does not always print well and tends to produce a glaring presence when displayed for a large audience.

Constructing a Resource Database

A resource database can be built on the same principle as the activity sequence database. By having each user do a standard worksheet that identifies resources and particular staff members, you have a tool for determining if a skill is actually going to be available for a task. It is possible, surely an oversight, that a task is scheduled but the person with the required skill is not available. This database, along with the activity sequence database, might assist you in identifying any such occurrences.

This database might include the following information:

- Person's name
- Available start date
- Available end data
- Associated task
- Group code
- Allocation of time
- Cost estimate
- Special requirements (training or equipment, one should enter none so it is noted that this was considered)

A person might require several rows in the database such as special requirements or more than one set of availability dates. By doing sorts you can easily identify all the team members that need training and the type of training required. There should be a standard on how special requirements are to be entered into the worksheet.

> **NOTE:**
> _____
>
> This database can be used to develop your annual budget. Perhaps another result is that you can see how your managers or team leaders plan to use staff members in a general manner. This database can also assist in developing capital requirements and the staff's time away from production for training.

Constructing a Spending Analysis Worksheet

A spending analysis is not a budget analysis. A spending analysis involves reviewing the total spending estimates for a project and each of the operational areas and the variance by month. A budget analysis would provide more detail in specifying budget lines.

An Excel worksheet would be constructed in the following manner:

1. Beginning on the first row, second column, enter the month in which the project begins. (This does not necessarily mean January.)

2. In the first column, second row, enter project adm. and then in the following rows enter each operational area.

3. Enter the estimates for monthly spending per group.

4. Make a summary row of estimates by month.

5. In the column after the months, make a summary of estimates by group.

6. Skip a row or two.

7. Copy the information from the first column.

8. As actual spending figures come in from each group, enter in each row.

9. Create a total spending row and spending to date column.

10. Skip a row or two.

11. Copy the information from the first column set.

12. In the cell next to *project adm.* enter *=sum* (cell of project adm. variance/B2).

13. To make the cell display percentage:

    — Click on *Format* on the Menu bar.

    — Click on *Number.*

    — Click on *Percentage.*

    — Check to see that Decimal Place box has 2.

    — Click *OK.*

When the variance is less than a hundred percent you keep going; but when it is greater than that and you are surprised, you need to resolve the issue *yesterday.* The practical goal is to have an overall variance percentage of less than a hundred.

NOTE:

A spending analysis is the detail required for verifying certain budget lines. One should consider the possibility of doing a monthly spending analysis of the IT budget. The skill set here is similar to balancing your personal checkbook. There is always the question, "Which is more complex to balance, my business budget or my personal budget?"

USE OF POWERPOINT TO MANAGE

A PowerPoint presentation can be used to state an attitude rather than a set of facts. In reality, there are many types of presentations. The following types of presentations are important to you as a manager:

- Executive summaries

- Team meetings

- Data-gathering meetings

- Customer presentations

In all cases, you should develop presentation standards. Using standards for presentations has its advantages:

- When a Web page is used, there is a common look and feel as to data presentation.

- Operational presentations can be merged into presentations for executive summaries with a minimal of administrative changes, or slides can be created quickly through cut-and-paste.

- Through experience, one can create new presentations quickly.

- Through experience, the audience can expect a certain consistency of informational flow.

To assist you in developing standards, there have been included with PowerPoint a number of templates. If you look at Presentations designs, there are seventeen. Some of the possible templates are the following:

- Professional

- Pulse

- Ribbons

If you look at Presentations, there are thirty-three templates. Five of these templates are directed toward project management:

- Project Overview (Standard) (two versions)
- Project Overview (Online)
- Project Status (Standard)
- Project Status (Online)

NOTE:

Some of these templates use a serif font such as Times New Roman. It is recommended that you use a sans serif (without curves) font such as Arial. Displayed type and Web pages are easier to read with a font such as Arial. In addition, you should consider any corporate graphic standards for PowerPoint presentations.

Executive Summary Presentations

An important function of an executive summary is to persuade. You need to present bottom-line issues in a top-level manner. Significant points of project status should be comprehensible quickly. You do not create a slide with details, but you use color. For example, if you wanted to present the status of all the operational areas as to schedule status, you could simply list them on a slide in various colors such as:

- Green—Ahead of schedule
- Black—On schedule
- Red—Behind schedule

With this technique, you do not have to have a chart with days ahead or behind; then you do an analysis. You get someone's attention in a hurry.

You can use the note function to give detailed information at the presentation or to give to the strategic manager after the presentation.

> **NOTE:**
>
> You could have one slide. The slide could be a pie chart with status percentages in green, black, and red.

Executive summary presentations should be short. If you have a half-hour presentation, plan to speak for no more than fifteen minutes with eight to twelve slides. If you do speak necessarily for the full half-hour, do not expect the audience to believe you have delivered a professional presentation.

There should be an emphasis on graphics rather than text. By using graphic capabilities of Excel, one can develop a professional-looking executive summary.

In addition, there is a simple thing you can to do to make an executive summary easier to present: Ask the strategic manager what the presentation's expectations are. I have seen an example where a corporate vice president defined his presentation expectations (standards) to his globally located directors. At the quarterly meetings, the presentations were consistent in tone and one could easily compare common situations (such as budget) among the different divisions.

Presentations for Meetings

A basic task of a manager is to manage and control events. You can use PowerPoint presentations for this task during meetings. While you should have sent out the meeting's agenda earlier, it is an excellent idea to have it as a presentation. By using the transition feature, you can bring up one point at a time. In addition, in the presentation you can give the time allocated for each item so that there is an even flow on all the items rather than having a rush at the end or running the meeting overtime.

As said earlier, use a sans serif font such as Arial. In addition, put only a few items per slide (a maximum of three bulleted items). What is readable on your monitor may not be readable in the conference room. Consider the size of the meeting room, perhaps a 14-point font should be a 24-point font.

For a project, the most important time for a PowerPoint presentation is at the first meeting. This presentation might set the tone for all further meetings. If it demonstrates that you know the direction of the project and points to the requirements to be considered to achieve success, you have made a big step forward.

In the first project presentation you need to outline needs in these 23 areas (project scope foundation):

1. Benchmarks

2. Performance

3. Validation

4. Risk

5. Data

    — Historical

    — Marketing

6. Time Parameters

7. Start Date

8. Milestones

9. End Date

10. Selection Criteria

11. Skills

    — Type

    — Level

12. Timelines

13. Resources

  — People (skills)

  — Equipment

  — Materials

14. Communications

15. Reports

16. Documentation

17. Training

18. Team

19. Customers

20. Support

21. Technical

22. Management

23. Marketing

The presentation should continue with 21 requirements for the scope definition:

1. Methodology

2. Resources

3. Integration

4. Communications

  — Who

  — When

  — How

  — Why

  — Where

5. Risk Analysis

6. Support services

7. Costing

8. Direct

   — Human

   — Time

   — Equipment

   — Materials

9. Indirect

10. Timing

11. Responsibilities

12. Support

13. Management

14. Customers

15. Technical

16. Quality control and assurance

17. Design

18. Development

19. Implementation

20. Testing

21. Validation

All other project meetings will be a variation on one or more of the areas above. There will be meetings for data gathering, for discussion status, and so forth, but this first meeting sets the framework for all the others to the project's conclusion.

Data-Gathering Presentations

You will have a number of data-gathering meetings. You can present a series of slides for a form to show how it should be filled out. Do not give one slide with one completed form, but a slide per box on the form or a set of related boxes.

You may also use presentations to stimulate brainstorming as to the types of data required. You can use either key words such as "code activities" or questions such as "What code activities are required for this piece of the product or project?"

Customer Presentations

The presentations should reflect what the customer is getting for funds expended. Unless there is a special request for it, minimize the technical. The presentations should reflect the concept of user-friendly. The basic principle is to use a minimum of words with large fonts and dynamic positive graphics. One should use graphics when possible to express the goals of the project. Do not give technical details about how a new server goes into the network for the training group; show a graphic of the IT network, highlighting the parts of the network that are impacted by the installation of the new server.

If the status of time is to be discussed, use Gantt charts with colors other than red and green.

Do not conclude from the above that you should speak down to the customer because they are not necessarily technically literate. This is far from the truth. Your presentations should reflect the customer's position, the one in need, and with the money.

USE OF WORD TO MANAGE

There is a tendency to think of the use of Word as a text editor (word processor) only. However, as a manager, you can use Word as a valuable communication tool for activity status. Beyond examples given, think of ways you can use it with e-mail. Status reports can be sent to all the staff members quickly.

Linking and Embedding Excel Tables into Word Project Reports

Summary tables discussed in the Excel worksheet examples could be either included or linked into a Word document. If you want to create a table, there are two methods:

- From the Menu bar choose *Table* ➔ *Insert Table*
- From the Standard bar click the *Insert Table* button (icon)

However, the inserting of a table may not be as important as the linking of an Excel worksheet to a Word document. Why is this feature important to you? This technique permits you to keep data updated on a regular basis without necessarily having to rewrite a new weekly or monthly status report. If modifications have to be done, you do the changes in the Excel worksheet rather than worrying about the editing process in Word. Again, you should link from the spending analysis worksheet, not from the document to the worksheet. This method permits you to generate a report without the consumption of a large amount of time.

Here are the nine basic steps for linking an Excel worksheet to a Word document:

1. Open the Excel worksheet that you want to link to the Word document.
2. Highlight (select) the data to be linked.
3. Click the *Copy* button or press *Ctrl* + C.
4. Open the Word document that is to receive the linked data.
5. Place the cursor at the location where data is to appear.
6. From the Menu bar choose *Edit* ➔ *Paste Special*.
7. In the *Paste Special* dialog box click the *Paste: Link* button.

8. Select the method whereby the worksheet is to appear in the Word document.

9. Click *OK*.

NOTE:

When the link between the worksheet and the document must be broken, it should be done from the worksheet file.

You can select any data or all of the data from an Excel worksheet to create a special status report.

The opposite of linking is embedding data. Embedding is the storing of a single Excel file's data in the Word document. In addition, embedding permits you to edit the data within the Word document.

NOTE:

The binder feature of Microsoft Office permits you to have one file with Word, PowerPoint, and Excel data in it. Sorry, you cannot do this using non-Microsoft products.

When should you use linking? When should you use embedding? Linking might be used for any of these reasons:

• File size needs to be small

• File needs to be updated dynamically

• Data needs to be controlled

NOTE:

All receivers of the file must have the same applications used to create the data and document (this means the version of the application might be significant).

Embedding might be used for any of these reasons:

- File is to be given to other staff members
- Convenience of a single file
- Data may be edited by a receiver of the file

NOTE:

Remember you lose control of data accuracy if you embed data in a document. In addition, a file's size with embeds becomes large quickly.

Using a Newsletter

The use of a newsletter is both creative and a positive method for presenting IT information. Any measurable data gathered and all the clearly defined activities and estimates mean absolutely nothing if they are not communicated to the correct people at the correct time. In addition, the direction of the communication might be lateral, upward, or downward.

The communication process is affected by at least five factors:

- Business environment
- Communication skills

- Credibility

- Frame of reference

- Staff member relationships

A newsletter might assist you in smoothing out the impact of these factors because the method of communication might play a significant role in the informational process. A newsletter may give you a more positive environment through which to present IT information than e-mail. In addition, e-mail can be more easily misinterpreted than a newsletter. Staff members can be praised for their successes in a more public manner. While a newsletter may take more time, it does look more professional than any e-mail.

A newsletter might be used to keep motivational slogans and important milestones to the forefront. In addition, production requirements might be presented using humorous cartoons or some dynamic graphic.

Using a Web Page

You might create a special Web page on your Intranet to have links to a server that includes documents, worksheets, and presentations. Word documents can quickly be converted to HTML documents by selecting *File* ➔ *Save as HTML.*

As an IT manager you should have staff members who are skilled in this technique. What is important here is the idea of using a special Web page for assisting in the communication process.

Using Word to Create Project Forms

Word can be used to create both printed and electronic forms and checklists. Is this valuable? On the CD-ROM that comes with this book there are a number of forms and checklists that might be used with your project. In addition, Chapter 23 includes self-assessment and checklist examples.

As has been shown in earlier chapters, you need to have checklists to standardize the gathering of data and to ensure that all the known basic data are identified and common processes are completed. You do not need elegant forms, but you do need professional-looking forms.

Any well-written book on Word should give you the dozen or so core steps it takes to create a form. It is important before you start to have either a sketched or an existing form to use in the creation of a new form.

SUMMARY OF YOUR USE OF SUPPORT SOFTWARE APPLICATIONS

One error will do you in quicker than anything else. It is not a too-small font. It is not a too-crowded slide. It is not a presentation without graphics. It is not a presentation with either too few or too many slides. *It is a misspelled word.* I have seen a group vice-president ignore the rest of a presentation once he saw a misspelled word.

The second danger is bad grammar, but you can get away with more than you think. Most will not realize that the Queen's English dictates "data are" rather than "data is," but be careful.

There are ten questions you need to consider when using office-type applications to do day-to-today operations or project management:

1. Are there standards available on output of the applications?
2. Do I have available someone skilled in one or more of the office-type applications?
3. How can I use a newsletter effectively?
4. How can I use a Web page for project management?
5. How effective can I be with different applications to get the most for the least amount of effort?
6. Is an application available for all to use?
7. What are the criteria for a customer status report presentation?

8. What are the criteria for an executive summary presentation?

9. What standards are required so operational inputs can be used easily and merged together to develop status reports?

10. What templates are required to create presentations?

On the CD-ROM

1. 22Overview.ppt—Chapter Overview

2. 22Excel.doc—Excel 97 Skills Self-Assessment

3. 22PPT.doc—PowerPoint 97 Skills Self-Assessment

4. 22Word.doc—Word 97 Skills Self-Assessment

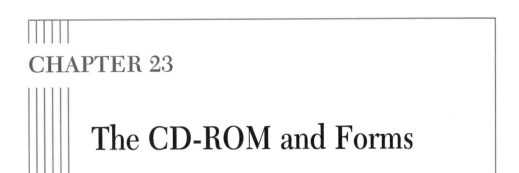

CHAPTER 23

The CD-ROM and Forms

Objectives: At the end of this chapter, you will be able to:

- Use the CD-ROM.
- List the types of documents on the CD-ROM.
- Describe and use the self-assessments and checklists that are related to the prior chapters in the book.

This chapter describes how to use the management skills documentation (forms, checklists, and presentations) templates found in the EXTRAS folder on the CD-ROM. On the following pages, documents and worksheets found on the CD-ROM are listed. In addition, all self-assessments and checklists that are in Word 97 format are included as handy references.

HOW TO USE THE CD-ROM

Windows and Macintosh Users: Open and read the README file in your word processor for complete installation instructions.

Acrobat Reader 4.0 (included in package) must be installed on your computer for this software to work properly.

System Requirements: Intel 486 or higher 16 MB RAM or higher (32 MB recommended) VGA/SVGA monitor, Mouse/pointing device, Windows 98/NT, Microsoft Excel, Adobe Acrobat Reader 4.0 (included).

Once Acrobat Reader has been installed and the electronic version of *Management Skills for IT Professionals* is running, complete instructions on running the program and using its navigational tools can be found in the HELP file by clicking on the ? icon, which appears on every page of the program.

CD-ROM EXTRAS FOLDER CONTENTS

The self-assessments, checklists, and worksheets are listed below by file name. Note the file name begins with the corresponding chapter number.

01whyqts.doc	Why am I at the level I am?
02SkillsList.doc	Skills Checklist
02General.doc	General Self-Assessment
02People.doc	Working with People Self-Assessment
03CInterview.doc	Ten Interview Questions for IS Consultants
03Interview.doc	Interviewing Self-Assessment
03JobSpec.xls	Job Specification
03QInterview.doc	Example Interview Questions
04Motivate.doc	Motivator Self-Assessment
04ExMots.doc	Example Motivators
04MotWkst.xls	Motivation Worksheet
05Creativity.doc	Three Assessments for Managing Creativity
05Decision.doc	Decision Making Self-Assessment
06Stress.doc	Handling Stress Self-Assessment
07Delegate.doc	Delegating Skills Self-Assessment
07Delegate.xls	Delegation Worksheet
08Feedback.doc	Feedback Skills Self-Assessment
08Final.xls	Termination Checklist
08Review.doc	Review Skills Self-Assessment
09TeamMgt.doc	Team Management Skills Self-Assessment

09TeamAsmt.xls	Team Assessment
10Organ.doc	Organizing Skills Self-Assessment
11Negotiate.doc	Negotiating Skills Self-Assessment
12Facil.doc	Facilitating Skills Self-Assessment
13Selling.doc	Selling Skills Self-Assessment
14Cust.doc	Customer Awareness Skills Self-Assessment
15Ven.doc	Vendor Awareness Skills Self-Assessment
16Communicate.doc	Oral Communication Skills Self-Assessment
17Communicate.doc	Written Communication Skills Self-Assessment
18Presentation.doc	Presentation Skills Self-Assessment
19TAsment1.doc	Time Management Self-Assessment
19TAsment2.doc	Time Management Self-Assessment of Meeting Skills
20QC.doc	Quality Control Awareness Skills Self-Assessment
20QCQts.doc	Quality Control and Deliverables Questions
21RAMSurvey.doc	Survey Questions for Creating a Risk Analysis Model
21Risk.doc	Risk Management Skills Self-Assessment
21RiskQts.doc	Risk Management Activities Questions
22Excel.doc	Excel 97 Skills Self-Assessment
22PPT.doc	PowerPoint 97 Skills Self-Assessment
22Word.doc	Word 97 Skills Self-Assessment

Also on the CD-ROM are overviews of Chapters 1 through 22 (nnOverview.ppt).

SELF-ASSESSMENTS AND CHECKLISTS

This section is a handy reference to documents as they appear on the CD-ROM. They are ordered by chapter.

Why Am I at the Level I Am?

You have achieved a level of success or wish to achieve a certain level of success. The following questions look at the skills level that you have or wish to acquire:

1. What technical skills do I have that have helped me to get this position?
2. What management skills do I have that have helped me to get this position?
3. What personal skills do I have that have helped me to get this position?
4. What are the corporate skill criteria that are used to determine success in the job that I now have?
5. What are the corporate skill criteria that are used to determine success in the job level that I now have?
6. What are the skill requirements for being an IT director? Manager? Team leader?
7. If I had to train a replacement what skills would I expect that person to have at the end of the training?
8. What skills do I see in my peers that I wish I had?
9. What skills do I see in upper management that demonstrate reasons for their success?
10. If I could design a management skills course what would I expect to be taught?

NOTES:

- You should answer these questions before reading the book and then again after reading the book.
- There are no correct or incorrect answers.
- Be as objective as possible.

Skills Checklist

The following is a list of 40 broad skill categories. You should determine your level of capability or expertise for each:

Adaptability

Analytical skills

Building influence

Business knowledge

Career planning

Comprehending peoples' actions

Conflict management

Control

Decision making

Delegation

Demonstrating experience

Demonstrating knowledge

Developing subordinates

Financial management

Formal interviewing

Formal presentations

Group problem solving

Hiring

Human relations

Informal interviewing

Interpersonal skills

Listening

Motivation of others

Motivation of self

Operational planning

Patience

Personnel evaluations

Planning goals

Problem solving

Remote management

Self-discipline

Strategic planning

Stress management

Tactical planning

Team management

Technical competence

Time management

Using power

Verbal communication

Written communication

NOTES:

- Identify the three strongest skill categories.
- Identify the three weakest skill categories.
- What do you think you should do to improve the three weakest categories?
- Read the applicable chapters in the book that primarily discuss the three weakest categories and then create an improvement plan.
- This list can be used in preparing evaluations of employees.

General Self-Assessment

For each of the following statements, enter a rating scale in the left-hand blank. If you cannot manage yourself, how do you expect to manage others?

RATING SCALE

0	Never	3	Frequently
1	Rarely	4	Consistently
2	Occasionally		

_____ 1. I confidently handle new tasks or approaches.

_____ 2. I have long-term career plans.

_____ 3. I periodically evaluate my skill set.

_____ 4. I seek feedback and react positively.

_____ 5. I seek to achieve excellence.

_____ 6. I seek a win-win situation when I compete.

_____ 7. I set aside time for self-improvement.

_____ 8. I look for new ideas.

_____ 9. I carefully analyze issues before making a decision.

_____ 10. I seek advice on business matters.

NOTES:

- These actions should be a part of your daily operations. You need to determine how these actions can be implemented to improve the IT environment.
- How you handle your own life reflects back on you. Others will notice what you do and what you do not do.
- Anything below a 3 should be improved.

Working with People Self-Assessment

For each of the following statements, enter a rating scale in the left-hand blank. No person is an island unto himself or herself.

RATING SCALE

0	Never	3	Frequently
1	Rarely	4	Consistently
2	Occasionally		

_____ 1. I evaluate people by the standards I meet.

_____ 2. I listen to others' ideas.

_____ 3. I positively evaluate others' opposing views.

_____ 4. I try to enhance people's pride in themselves.

_____ 5. I seek to find the right job for the right person.

_____ 6. I make myself available to others.

_____ 7. I am concerned that employees get quality training.

_____ 8. I motivate by example.

_____ 9. I seek feedback on my job from employees.

_____ 10. I seek to identify talent and then promote it.

NOTES:

• The core of all skills is how you interact with people.
• As you treat one person, so will all the other people take notice.
• Anything below a 3 should be improved.

Ten Interview Questions for IS Consultants

For each of the following questions include a specific example of how you would handle the situation:

1. In your opinion what is the best way to communicate with people?

2. What types of time management techniques do you use in a consulting environment?

3. How do you make your decisions? How do you assist others in making decisions?

4. What techniques do you use to resolve problems?

5. What techniques do you use to motivate your customers?

6. Do you have assistants? What techniques do you use to ensure that the customer is involved in the consulting process?

7. How do you assist the customer in clarifying the project goals?

8. What abilities or expertise do you have that can assist in ensuring this project is achieved?

9. Do you work with the team or use an "outsider's" view of the situation?

10. What techniques do you use to resolve differences between the customers?

NOTES:

- Put adequate space between the questions so you can write down the responses.
- Prior to any interviewing write down answers you would like to hear as benchmarks.
- After all interviews do an analysis of the responses question by question; that is, analyze all responses to question 1 first. Use a plus-minus (for example -3 to +3) system in comparing a consultant's answers with your answers. Then add the pluses and minuses to get an overall response score.
- You might let others read the responses, who were not present for the interviews.
- Question 8 is where you get to the required technical qualifications. It is very important that you have a set of measurable criteria. "Know Java" is not a measurable objective.

Interviewing Self-Assessment

For each of the following statements, enter a rating scale in the left-hand blank. To find the best answers in the shortest time is always difficult when it comes to people.

RATING SCALE

0	Never	3	Frequently
1	Rarely	4	Consistently
2	Occasionally		

_____ 1. I prepare when I have to handle an interview.

_____ 2. I evaluate the job description.

_____ 3. I consider various recruiting methods.

_____ 4. I select an appropriate location for the interview.

_____ 5. I involve other people before an interview.

_____ 6. I involve other people during an interview.

_____ 7. I involve other people after an interview.

_____ 8. I encourage the candidate to talk about prior experiences.

_____ 9. I ask about gaps in employment history.

_____ 10. I complete the interview process before making a decision.

_____ 11. I make notes during an interview with the candidate's permission.

_____ 12. I assess whether the candidate will fit into the group culture.

_____ 13. I ask candidates how they will benefit the group.

_____ 14. I stay objective during the interview.

_____ 15. I seek to determine a balance of a candidate's strengths and
           weaknesses.

NOTES:

- A winning interview requires preparation.
- Involving others in the interview process demonstrates a level of trust.
- Anything below a 3 should be improved.

Job Specification

Excel format on CD-ROM.

Example Interview Questions

1. What are your current duties and responsibilities?
2. What is a typical workday for you?
3. What caused you to apply for this job?
4. What are your views about this job?
5. What are your expectations from this job?
6. What are some of the problems you had to resolve in your present position?
7. What experiences have you had that you think may benefit you in this job?
8. What do you like best about your present position?
9. Why did you choose this career?
10. Is there any additional training that you might require in fulfilling this job?
11. If accepted for this job, when could you come to work?
12. What is your long-term career goal?
13. How did you change your present job's duties and responsibilities?
14. What do you like least about your present position?
15. This job requires that you do X, how would you handle this requirement?
16. What do think are your primary accomplishments in your career?
17. How do think you will benefit the IS group?
18. What is the culture like at your present job?
19. How could you contribute immediately to this job?
20. What other things do you think should be known about your career?

Motivator Self-Assessment

For each of the following statements, enter a rating scale in the left-hand blank. If you are not motivated to achieve a goal, how can you motivate others to achieve the same goal?

RATING SCALE

0	Never	3	Frequently
1	Rarely	4	Consistently
2	Occasionally		

_____ 1. I try persuasion rather than force.

_____ 2. I try to give full information to my employees.

_____ 3. I involve people in issues as soon as possible.

_____ 4. I seek a balance between independence and control.

_____ 5. I use reasonable benchmarks to stimulate work.

_____ 6. I look for ways to remove obstacles so there can be success.

_____ 7. I seek feedback and react accordingly.

_____ 8. I encourage initiative.

_____ 9. I seek ways for people to complete a task.

_____ 10. I delegate tasks that I do not have to do.

_____ 11. I find ways for people to work to their full potential.

_____ 12. I ask before making major changes.

_____ 13. I make assignments to develop people.

_____ 14. I seek opportunities for change.

_____ 15. I correct failures; I do not place blame.

NOTES:

- Each person is motivated in different ways. In addition, groups are motivated differently.
- When you hear your people wishing to win the lottery so they can do something else, you need to find out how you can be motivating those people.
- Anything below a 3 should be improved.

Example Motivators

1. Learn what a person's mode of operation is.
2. Be interested in each person.
3. Encourage each person's ideas.
4. Give each person opportunities for professional growth.
5. Give each person opportunities to be creative.
6. Keep a motivation worksheet on each person.
7. Base performance expectations on measurable benchmarks.
8. Professionally challenge each person.
9. Give each person realistic responsibilities with associated authority.
10. Keep people informed of the goals of the IT group.
11. Give prompt answers.
12. Empower people.
13. Give credit openly when due.
14. Be accessible.
15. Give training to enhance personal growth.
16. Be supportive.
17. Assist in resolving work problems.
18. Direct people to experts on personal problems.
19. Give training to enhance technical skills.
20. Give training to enhance personal skills.

Motivation Worksheet

Excel form on CD-ROM.

Three Assessments for Managing Creativity

For each of the following statements, enter a rating scale in the left-hand blank. Can you tell the difference between creativity and random chaotic thinking?

RATING SCALE

0	Never	3	Frequently
1	Rarely	4	Consistently
2	Occasionally		

Routine Problems

_____ 1. I can clearly and precisely define a problem.

_____ 2. I define the problem before looking for a solution.

_____ 3. I look for alternative solutions rather than one.

_____ 4. I consider the results and consequences of each solution.

_____ 5. I do research for data to achieve the most effective and efficient solution.

_____ 6. I use a problem-solving process rather than a hit-and-miss technique.

_____ 7. I revise a solution if it does not seem to be effective or efficient.

Difficult Problems

_____ 1. I use the steps in solving a routine problem as a foundation for a further solution.

_____ 2. I work with more than one potential solution.

_____ 3. I try to be flexible with the use of potential solutions.

____ 4. I look for a commonality or pattern among the potential solutions.

____ 5. I look for the nature of the problem rather than considering an obvious view.

____ 6. I consider both the irrational and rational possibilities of the problem.

____ 7. I look for analogies to the problem for potential solutions.

____ 8. I consider that my initial view may be completely incorrect.

____ 9. I break the large down into smaller manageable parts.

____ 10. I try to apply known problem-solving techniques to achieve a solution.

Fostering Creativity in Others

____ 1. I try to develop opportunities for employees to work without constraints.

____ 2. I listen with an open mind to what employees have to say about solving a problem.

____ 3. I use the strange position to challenge people who live within the walls.

____ 4. I use the principle that informed rule breaking is a valid technique.

____ 5. I use outsiders to stimulate ideas.

NOTES:

- There has to be a balance between permitting creativity and the bottom line.
- Creativity cannot be permitted to change project goals, only the methods for achieving them.
- Anything below a 3 should be improved.

Decision Making Self-Assessment

For each of the following statements, enter a rating scale in the left-hand blank. Your form of decision making is uniquely different from anyone else's. Your decisions can have a definite impact on creativity.

RATING SCALE

0	Never	3	Frequently
1	Rarely	4	Consistently
2	Occasionally		

_____ 1. I make timely decisions and ensure that they are implemented.

_____ 2. I permit others to make decisions that I am not required to make.

_____ 3. I do an analysis of the situation before making a decision.

_____ 4. I make my decisions in the context of the corporate environment.

_____ 5. I consider alternatives before making a final decision.

_____ 6. I identify objective criteria for making decisions.

_____ 7. I seek the involvement of others in the decision-making process.

_____ 8. I consult others in making decisions.

_____ 9. I seek support for my decisions.

_____ 10. I use computers in assisting me to make decisions.

NOTES:
- How do you support decision making in your group?
- How you handle your decisions is noticed by others. Your business decisions rarely impact only yourself.
- Anything below a 3 should be improved.

Handling Stress Self-Assessment

For each of the following statements, enter a rating scale in the left-hand blank. You need to handle your stress to manage conflict.

RATING SCALE

0	Never	3	Frequently
1	Rarely	4	Consistently
2	Occasionally		

_____ 1. I am aware of the corporation's policy on stress management.

_____ 2. I work in terms of correct and incorrect, rather than right and wrong.

_____ 3. I look for the positive rather than the negative.

_____ 4. I do notice negative changes in myself.

_____ 5. I seek to correct a problem rather than placing blame.

_____ 6. I believe I have time to stop and smell the roses periodically.

_____ 7. I am comfortable with new situations.

_____ 8. I take advice from peers.

_____ 9. I take time to have lunch with peers.

_____ 10. I seek to resolve issues rather than waiting to have a confrontation.

_____ 11. I accept my professional limitations.

_____ 12. I accept that things do not happen immediately.

_____ 13. I do not accept failure as a solution.

_____ 14. I delegate tasks to others that are not required of me.

_____ 15. I accept pauses during the work day as positive events.

NOTES:

- Your stress only negatively adds to a conflict.
- How you handle your stress reflects on your demeanor. Others will notice when your face reflects stress.
- Anything below a 3 should be improved.

Delegating Skills Self-Assessment

For each of the following statements, enter a rating scale in the left-hand blank. Delegation means letting others do what is not required of you.

RATING SCALE

0   Never   3   Frequently
1   Rarely   4   Consistently
2   Occasionally

_____ 1. I let people to whom I delegate authority know that I trust them.

_____ 2. I am loyal to the people to whom I delegate authority.

_____ 3. I prepare people for delegated authority.

_____ 4. I ensure that a specific responsibility belongs to a specific person.

_____ 5. I provide appropriate backup support.

_____ 6. I objectively evaluate who can have authority.

_____ 7. I encourage those with authority to make their own decisions.

_____ 8. I seek to give the correct amount of authority to the correct person.

_____ 9. I review periodically with a person how delegated authority is being handled.

_____ 10. I remove authority only after all alternatives have been considered.

NOTES:

- Delegating is probably the most difficult of skills. It requires trust.
- How you handle delegation is important to all other people's skill sets, such as creativity.
- Anything below a 3 should be improved.

Delegation Worksheet

Excel format on CD-ROM.

Feedback Skills Self-Assessment

For each of the following statements, enter a rating scale in the left-hand blank. Feedback is a validation skill. This assessment is from you giving feedback rather than receiving it.

RATING SCALE

0   Never   3   Frequently

1   Rarely   4   Consistently

2   Occasionally

_____   1. I always suggest alternatives.

_____   2. I set aside a time when the feedback will not be interrupted.

_____   3. I seek to counsel rather than to dictate.

_____   4. I comprehend when it is an appropriate time to give feedback.

_____   5. I have regular sessions for feedback.

_____   6. I give the other person the opportunity to speak.

_____   7. I relate feedback to a standard that has been achieved or unachieved.

_____   8. I try to put forth my interests in what the other person has to say.

_____   9. I give negative feedback in a manner equal to positive feedback.

_____ 10. I try to strengthen a relationship even when negative feedback is given.

_____ 11. I try not to speak down to the person receiving the feedback.

_____ 12. I accept new information during the feedback.

____ 13. I distinguish between coaching and counseling feedback.

____ 14. I give specific feedback rather the type that is general.

____ 15. I use descriptions of events and their results or consequences.

NOTES:

- Be honest and reply with integrity.
- The big question is "Are you supportive?"
- Anything below a 3 should be improved.

Termination Checklist

Excel format on CD-ROM.

Review Skills Self-Assessment

For each of the following statements, enter a rating scale in the left-hand blank. The review process is probably one of the most stressful events for both the giver and receiver during a business year.

RATING SCALE

0	Never	3	Frequently
1	Rarely	4	Consistently
2	Occasionally		

_____ 1. I accept feedback.

_____ 2. I seek to find out performance strengths and weaknesses from others on the person being reviewed.

_____ 3. I have techniques to handle ambiguous situations.

_____ 4. I am conscious of potentially contentious areas.

_____ 5. I know I have to control my temper in delicate situations.

_____ 6. I seek to find the positive in the negative.

_____ 7. I manage for success not failure.

_____ 8. I recognize my personal management styles in handling reviews.

_____ 9. I comprehend that my interpersonal needs can impact a review.

_____ 10. I have to accept the results and consequences of the review.

NOTES:

- The review should not be a one-time event filled with surprises.
- The big question is "Are you objective?"
- Anything below a 3 should be improved.

Team Management Skills Self-Assessment

For each of the following statements, enter a rating scale in the left-hand blank. Team Management is a combination of individual and group management.

RATING SCALE

0	Never	3	Frequently
1	Rarely	4	Consistently
2	Occasionally		

____ 1. I use different team strategies for success.

____ 2. I work with the team, not oversee the team.

____ 3. I recognize that success belongs to the team, while failure is mine.

____ 4. I seek ways to publicly praise team efforts.

____ 5. I listen objectively to what team members have to say.

____ 6. I seek to find ways to motivate indifference.

____ 7. I try to be pro-active rather than reactive.

____ 8. I seek to have a professional feedback environment.

____ 9. I recognize my spoken and body languages could generate either optimism or pessimism in the team.

____ 10. I seek to create an environment of openness rather than one of proprietary ideas.

NOTES:

- Team management is fundamentally working with people skills rather than technical skills.
- The big question is "Do you speak the language of all the team members?"
- Anything below a 3 should be improved.

Team Assessment

Excel format on CD-ROM.

Organizing Skills Self-Assessment

For each of the following statements, enter a rating scale in the left-hand blank. Organizational skills are an awareness of a corporation's infrastructure that includes people structures, culture, and intangibles such as integrity.

RATING SCALE

0	Never	3	Frequently
1	Rarely	4	Consistently
2	Occasionally		

_____ 1. I am aware of the changes in the corporate infrastructure that affect the IS group.

_____ 2. I think in terms of people configurations, interactive systems, groups, and teams.

_____ 3. I direct my group toward a common goal.

_____ 4. I use written and oral communication to gain interpersonal influence.

_____ 5. I comprehend corporate group boundaries and use them for the good of my group.

_____ 6. I maintain cooperative relationships with other groups.

_____ 7. I set objectives for my group.

_____ 8. I seek to have a professional feedback environment.

_____ 9. I am self-motivated.

_____ 10. I am achievement oriented.

_____ 11. I try to change the status quo.

____ 12. I am confident of my organizational skills.

____ 13. I am an interpreter of events.

____ 14. I seek to convince others in such a manner that the idea appears to be theirs.

____ 15. I can make difficult decisions.

NOTES:

- As an organizer, one has to be careful about any other label placed on her or him such as boss, tyrant, or negotiator.
- An organizer is more an "us" person than an "I" person, but highly self-motivated.
- If you want to be perceived as an organizer, anything below a 3 should be improved.

Negotiating Skills Self-Assessment

For each of the following statements, enter a rating scale in the left-hand blank. Negotiating does not mean I win, you lose.

RATING SCALE

0	Never	3	Frequently
1	Rarely	4	Consistently
2	Occasionally		

_____ 1. I prepare for a negotiation.

_____ 2. I have established objectives when I negotiate.

_____ 3. I use negotiating tactics appropriate to the goals.

_____ 4. I do have a negotiating strategy.

_____ 5. I use plain language in a negotiation rather than technical language.

_____ 6. I identify realistic goals and schedules.

_____ 7. I present a logical argument for a negotiation.

_____ 8. I work in a negotiation so both parties win.

_____ 9. I do not make an opening offer.

_____ 10. I negotiate step by step.

NOTES:

- Negotiating goes on all the time, mostly informally.
- How you handle your negotiations reflects on how your team perceives your abilities. If you let the other party, a customer, win completely, what type of group stresses can happen?
- Anything below a 3 should be improved.

Facilitating Skills Self-Assessment

For each of the following statements, enter a rating scale in the left-hand blank. Facilitating skills are an awareness of diversity in individuals and groups, and accepting diversity is a cornerstone of all personal interactions.

RATING SCALE

0	Never	3	Frequently
1	Rarely	4	Consistently
2	Occasionally		

_____ 1. I respect others for their differences.

_____ 2. I am supportive.

_____ 3. I listen to others.

_____ 4. I make allowances for the differences in others.

_____ 5. I use individual uniqueness to enhance the whole.

_____ 6. I use two-way communication.

_____ 7. I set objectives for my group.

_____ 8. I am pro-active in resolving conflicts caused by differences.

_____ 9. I accept ambiguity when necessary.

_____ 10. I try to ensure all have the opportunity to speak in meetings.

_____ 11. I identify processes that might hamper diversity as a positive influence on my group's growth.

_____ 12. I seek to make things easier for my group through diverse opportunities.

_____ 13. I see myself as a mentor.

_____ 14. I believe facilitating is more than just "touch and feel."

_____ 15. I think that an aspect of diversity such as having technical skills
           can hamper personal interrelations.

NOTES:

- As a facilitator one has to be careful as to any other label placed on her or
  him such as mother or father figures.
- A facilitator accepts the changing colors of sunlight and the shades of the
  social structure.
- If you want to be perceived as a facilitator, anything below a 3 should be
  improved.

Selling Skills Self-Assessment

For each of the following statements, enter a rating scale in the left-hand blank. You are always a salesperson each time you put forth an idea for others to accept.

RATING SCALE

0	Never	3	Frequently
1	Rarely	4	Consistently
2	Occasionally		

_____ 1. I develop a plan before talking to a customer.

_____ 2. I identify the customer's needs so I can approach them for success.

_____ 3. I seek new ways to make a sale better.

_____ 4. I negotiate so all parties win.

_____ 5. I change my sales approach according to the customer's reactions.

_____ 6. I do research to improve my selling skills.

_____ 7. I do presentations based on the audience.

_____ 8. I consider possible objections by the customer prior to any meeting.

_____ 9. I try to resolve issues in a timely manner.

_____ 10. I seek advice on making a sale that can impact the corporation and the IS group.

NOTES:

- Selling is a skill that is required in each successful IT manager's skill set.
- You are selling each time you give a presentation, interview a person, or review a person.
- Anything below a 3 should be improved.

Customer Awareness Skills Self-Assessment

For each of the following statements, enter a rating scale in the left-hand blank. Working with customers—that is, almost if not all the people in the corporation—is a unique opportunity of nearly all IT managers because of the electronic age of networking.

RATING SCALE

0	Never	3	Frequently
1	Rarely	4	Consistently
2	Occasionally		

_____ 1. I develop a plan before talking to a customer.

_____ 2. I identify the customer's needs so I can approach them for success.

_____ 3. I talk to customers on neutral ground when possible.

_____ 4. I negotiate so all parties win.

_____ 5. I change my tactics according to the customer's reactions.

_____ 6. I strive to have criteria of excellence that will result in customer satisfaction.

_____ 7. I do presentations based on the customer's needs not my own.

_____ 8. I consider possible objections by the customer prior to any meeting.

_____ 9. I try to resolve issues in a timely manner.

_____ 10. I seek to get clear measurable definitions of the requirements of the customer.

NOTES:

- Customer relationships require the art of being an organizer, negotiator, facilitator, and most of all, salesperson.
- You need to identify the importance of customer views.
- Anything below a 3 should be improved.

Vendor Awareness Skills Self-Assessment

For each of the following statements, enter a rating scale in the left-hand blank. Working with vendors you are the customer and you should be treated as you treat your customers.

RATING SCALE

0	Never	3	Frequently
1	Rarely	4	Consistently
2	Occasionally		

_____ 1. I develop a set of product criteria before talking to a vendor.

_____ 2. I expect the vendor to have or develop product documentation that meets my requirements.

_____ 3. I get resumes based on my needs from vendors before using their consultants.

_____ 4. I negotiate so all parties win.

_____ 5. I expect vendors to have security solutions for their products when applicable.

_____ 6. I expect to be told of the vendor's quality control process.

_____ 7. I develop interview questions prior to a discussion with a vendor.

_____ 8. I expect to hear from vendors how they can benefit my company.

_____ 9. I expect a vendor to resolve issues in a timely manner.

_____ 10. I give clear measurable product requirements to the vendors.

NOTES:

- Vendor relationships require two-way communication based on trust.
- You need to identify the importance of why a vendor seeks to do business with your company.
- Anything below a 3 should be improved.

Oral Communication Skills Self-Assessment

For each of the following statements, enter a rating scale in the left-hand blank. Once something is said, it cannot be erased.

RATING SCALE

0	Never	3	Frequently
1	Rarely	4	Consistently
2	Occasionally		

____ 1. I speak to the listener.

____ 2. I speak using plain language.

____ 3. I try to select the correct message for the situation.

____ 4. I speak objectively.

____ 5. I try to think before I speak.

____ 6. I speak constructively.

____ 7. I use the appropriate presentation mode.

____ 8. I recognize that speaking and body language go hand in hand.

____ 9. I speak to any internal and external audience as is appropriate.

____ 10. I do serious research before giving a presentation.

NOTES:
- Oral communication is unsafe written communication.
- What you say becomes a translated message.
- Anything below a 3 should be improved.

Written Communication Skills Self-Assessment

For each of the following statements, enter a rating scale in the left-hand blank. Selecting the correct words at the correct time is the skill, all else is commentary.

RATING SCALE

0 Never	3 Frequently
1 Rarely	4 Consistently
2 Occasionally	

_____ 1. I write to the reader.

_____ 2. I write using plain language.

_____ 3. I try to select the correct message for the situation.

_____ 4. I write objectively.

_____ 5. I think before I write.

_____ 6. I write constructively.

_____ 7. I use the appropriate writing medium.

_____ 8. I take notes to be effective.

_____ 9. I write to any internal and external audience as is appropriate.

_____ 10. I do serious research before writing a proposal.

NOTES:

- Written communication is slow oral communication.
- What you write is the message.
- Anything below a 3 should be improved.

Presentation Skills Self-Assessment

For each of the following statements, enter a rating scale in the left-hand blank. The art of a good presentation is the art of a good sale.

RATING SCALE

0	Never	3	Frequently
1	Rarely	4	Consistently
2	Occasionally		

_____ 1. I do research prior to doing a presentation.

_____ 2. I practice my presentation so it sounds fresh.

_____ 3. I give organized presentations.

_____ 4. I give the audience time at the end of the presentation to ask questions.

_____ 5. I seek an attention grabber at the beginning of the presentation.

_____ 6. I make eye contact with the audience.

_____ 7. I give an evenly paced presentation.

_____ 8. I answer questions precisely.

_____ 9. I identify personal mannerisms that might distract the audience.

_____ 10. I use visual aids when appropriate.

NOTES:

- A presentation is the blending of oral and written communication skills.
- You only have one time to make the presentation.
- Anything below a 3 should be improved.

Time Management Self-Assessment

For each of the following statements, enter a rating scale in the left-hand blank. If you cannot time manage yourself, how do you expect to time manage others?

RATING SCALE

0	Never	3	Frequently
1	Rarely	4	Consistently
2	Occasionally		

_____ 1. I have a place for everything.

_____ 2. I list daily tasks.

_____ 3. I set deadlines for myself.

_____ 4. I do something productive while waiting.

_____ 5. I work on the principle that 20 percent of my work produces 80 percent of the results.

_____ 6. I look for ways to improve my effectiveness.

_____ 7. I finish at least one task a day.

_____ 8. I track my time in a log.

_____ 9. I divide projects into achievable parts.

_____ 10. I establish priorities for my tasks.

NOTES:

- These actions can be moved into daily operations. You need to determine how these actions can be implemented for each general IT position. How can a programmer use these actions? How can customer service personnel use these actions?
- How you handle your time reflects on your management skills. Others will notice when you say "I am busy, keep it short" or your face reflects stress.
- Anything below a 3 should be improved.

Time Management Self-Assessment of Meeting Skills

For each of the following statements, enter a rating scale in the left-hand blank. If you cannot manage your own time, how do you expect to time manage others?

RATING SCALE

0	Never	3	Frequently
1	Rarely	4	Consistently
2	Occasionally		

_____ 1. I start meetings on time.

_____ 2. I have a written agenda and reach closure on each item.

_____ 3. I hold short meetings standing up.

_____ 4. I do not hold important meetings at the end of the day.

_____ 5. I end all meetings on time.

_____ 6. I send out an agenda prior to a meeting.

_____ 7. I stick to the agenda.

_____ 8. I do not have unnecessary meetings.

_____ 9. I have someone take notes.

_____ 10. I write the final notes promptly after the meeting.

NOTES:
- Meetings are one of the worst eaters of time.
- Necessary meetings are one of the best places to manage time.
- Remember a meeting of one hour with eight people is not one-hour lost, but one workday.
- Unnecessary meetings cost more than time.
- Anything below a 3 should be improved.

Quality Control Awareness Skills Self-Assessment

For each of the following statements, enter a rating scale in the left-hand blank. An IT manager probably has available more external quality control standards and benchmarks than any other manager.

RATING SCALE

0	Never	3	Frequently
1	Rarely	4	Consistently
2	Occasionally		

_____ 1. I have an active quality control program within my group.

_____ 2. I use peer reviews.

_____ 3. I look for potential areas where errors can happen in an IT project.

_____ 4. I consider the cost consequences of errors.

_____ 5. I use system tools to manage system quality control.

_____ 6. I use my quality control program in selling my group to customers.

_____ 7. I review my quality control program.

_____ 8. I use objective quality control benchmarks to determine performance.

_____ 9. I develop measurable goals for IT projects.

_____ 10. I expect a high level of quality control from vendors.

NOTES:
- A quality control program can be the keystone of a user-friendly program of excellence.
- Quality control and high performance go hand in hand.
- Anything below a 4 should be improved.

Quality Control and Deliverables Questions

1. Have quality standards been made consistent?

2. Has a comprehensive quality control program been defined including standards and benchmarks?

3. Has the quality process been cost estimated and budgeted?

4. Have the quality control events been included at appropriate milestones?

5. What are the criteria for documenting quality control activities?

6. What are the quality control procedures that ensure correct sequencing?

7. What are the quality control procedures that need to be in the activity plan?

8. What are the standards and benchmarks for quality control?

9. What is the necessary time for quality validation?

10. What quality control policies, benchmarks, or standards have to be followed?

Questions on a Deliverable

1. Does documentation correctly state technical requirements?

2. Does it meet appropriate standards?

3. Does it meet corporate benchmarks?

4. Does it meet functional requirements?

5. Does it meet operational requirements?

6. Does it meet protocol requirements?

7. Does it meet security requirements?

8. Does it technically fulfill project goals?

9. Does the help function assist the customer in resolving technical issues?

10. Have training courses been developed to cover technical issues?

NOTES:

- These questions should not be answered with a simple yes or no, but with fully stated answers.
- The first set of questions should be answered on at least a quarterly basis.
- The second set of questions should be asked when reviewing development status and before any deliverable is made to a customer or put into production.

Survey Questions for Creating a Risk Analysis Model

1. Are there "slippage" dates for any project schedule?

2. Are there standards or benchmarks for comparing activity durations?

3. Has a critical path been established for each project?

4. Are the dates, equipment, and resources available from all vendors and consultants?

5. Have all documentation activity sequences for all projects been identified?

6. Have all milestones for all projects been identified?

7. Have all operational activity sequences for all projects been identified?

8. Have all quality control points for all projects been identified?

9. Have all revenue dates been identified?

10. Have all training activity sequences for all projects been identified?

11. Have critical equipment requirement dates been established for all projects?

12. Have critical material requirement dates been established for all projects?

13. Have deliverable dates been identified for all projects?

14. Have hardware infrastructure benchmarks (interoperability, portability, and so forth) been identified?

15. Have indirect cost estimates been identified?

16. Have operational cost estimates been identified?

17. Have skill level benchmarks been identified for all projects?

18. Have skills availabilities been identified for all projects?

19. Have software infrastructure benchmarks (configuration, compatibility, and so forth) been identified?

20. Have status report dates been identified for all projects?

NOTES:

- These questions should not be answered with a simple yes or no, but with specific examples of status. For example, all skill levels available and not available should be listed.
- This survey should be done in association with the quarterly reviews of the budget.

Risk Management Skills Self-Assessment

For each of the following statements, enter a rating scale in the left-hand blank. To an IT manager a risk to the system is a minute-to-minute situation rather than a potential event.

RATING SCALE

0	Never	3	Frequently
1	Rarely	4	Consistently
2	Occasionally		

_____ 1. I use network and Internet standards to define my system processes.

_____ 2. I use a set of publicly distributed security policies.

_____ 3. I use external and internal technical benchmarks to define system performance.

_____ 4. I use external and internal technical benchmarks to define the performance of employees.

_____ 5. I use system tools to manage system performance.

_____ 6. I use audits and auditing to limit risks to the system.

_____ 7. I use a risk management program.

_____ 8. I assess a risk to see if it can be turned into an opportunity.

_____ 9. I develop measurable criteria to define a system risk.

_____ 10. I evaluate my system periodically to determine potential system risks.

NOTES:

- Risk management is a tool to put light in the closet to keep out the monsters.
- A risk is an event that can cause serious harm to the system that can start with such an event as password abuse.
- Anything below a 4 should be improved.

Risk Management Activities Questions

1. Are there any training requirements for risk management?

2. Do project schedules have appropriate links from the quality control schedule to other areas of the group schedule?

3. What are the criteria for risk management that may impact activities?

4. What are the direct-cost estimates for risk management activities?

5. What are the documentation requirements and standards for risk management?

6. What are the essential project activities managing risks?

7. What are the resources required for risk management?

8. What are the skills and their levels required for risk management?

9. What are my annual time estimates for risk management?

10. What are my procedures, standards, or policies that govern risk management?

Excel 97 Skills Self-Assessment

For each of the following statements, enter a rating scale in the left-hand blank. Spreadsheets can be used effectively to establish "what if" scenarios.

RATING SCALE

0	Never	3	Frequently
1	Rarely	4	Consistently
2	Occasionally		

_____ 1. I use toolbars instead of menu options.

_____ 2. I use Excel spreadsheets to develop "what if" scenarios for IT projects.

_____ 3. I use Excel to develop management forms.

_____ 4. I use Excel to develop technical reports for upper management.

_____ 5. I use Excel to develop graphic presentations.

_____ 6. I use Excel to manage financial scenarios.

_____ 7. I use Excel to account monthly for personnel activities such as training, vacation time, project activities, etc.

_____ 8. I use the Chart Wizard.

_____ 9. I use a workbook when I have multiple related worksheets.

_____ 10. I use Excel for time accounting for the usage of people, hardware, and software.

NOTES:

• Excel can be used to develop charts for presentations where one chart can replace many textual slides.
• An excellent management skill is accounting for time for training, customer service, programming, maintenance, etc.
• Anything below a 3 should be improved.

PowerPoint 97 Skills Self-Assessment

For each of the following statements, enter a rating scale in the left-hand blank. Half of a sale is an effective presentation.

RATING SCALE

0	Never	3	Frequently
1	Rarely	4	Consistently
2	Occasionally		

____ 1. I use sans serif (without curving strokes) for my presentations.

____ 2. I use no more than three bullet items per slide.

____ 3. I use AutoContent Wizard to assist in developing new presentations.

____ 4. I use backgrounds that do not distract from the presentation.

____ 5. I use the toolbars rather than the menu options.

____ 6. I use the outline view to develop my presentations.

____ 7. I use the slide sorter view to assist in editing the flow of a presentation.

____ 8. I use a font size that is appropriate for viewing by the audiences.

____ 9. I use the notes page view to assist me in giving a presentation.

____ 10. I use printing options to create handouts with two or more slides per page.

NOTES:

- PowerPoint includes a number of templates to assist in developing presentations more easily.
- Probably the biggest presentation error besides misspelled words is the poor use of colors for fonts and backgrounds such as the use of yellow or glaring color shades.
- Anything below a 3 should be improved.

Word 97 Skills Self-Assessment

For each of the following statements, enter a rating scale in the left-hand blank. You can impress your **IT** group by doing documents that go beyond the usual and sometimes they are easier to do than the normal process.

RATING SCALE

0	Never	3	Frequently
1	Rarely	4	Consistently
2	Occasionally		

_____ 1. I use Word 97 document templates (faxes, memos, and reports).

_____ 2. I use Word 97 for attachments in my e-mails.

_____ 3. I have standards for my group for writing reports.

_____ 4. I use hyperlinks in my documents.

_____ 5. I use the spelling and grammar tool.

_____ 6. I use the language tool.

_____ 7. I use toolbars other than standard and formatting.

_____ 8. I use the toolbars rather than the menu options.

_____ 9. I use newsletters to provide information.

_____ 10. I use views other than normal to develop documents.

NOTES:

- Word 97 has many options that can make one's writing easier.
- The use of Word is important in writing activity logs that can be edited and sent on to upper management when necessary.
- Anything below a 3 should be improved.

Glossary

Ability is the capacity to achieve or to perform and is enhanced through training.

Accommodation is the negative skill of satisfying the needs of other parties while ignoring your own and results usually in a lose-lose situation.

Action-oriented is an orientation to doing rather than planning.

Advising is giving general rather than specific directions; evaluating, giving an option, or instructing.

Avoiding is the negative skill of sidestepping an issue to avoid conflict.

Brainstorming is the technique of first identifying alternatives in an unordered process and seeking a common resolution from the alternatives.

Centrality is a power position within a group, perhaps even within a team, where information can flow from established positions on issues.

Charismatic leaders are leaders who are full of the "spirit," which is actually self-assurance and self-confidence.

Closed questions are questions asked during an interview to restrict a candidate's position and is effective when time is limited or when an answer has to be clarified.

Coaching is the sports metaphor for giving advice, stating information or setting standards to a subordinate (one never coaches a management superior).

Cognitive style is a style where the imparting of information is primary.

Cognitive style strategies are problem-solving patterns that emphasize the methods that one uses to receive, process, and store knowledge.

Collaborating is a technique of conflict management that tries to satisfy everyone.

Commitment is usually a positive skill that establishes a person's point of view or solution to an issue (see compression).

Communication is oral or written transfer of data or information between individuals.

Competitive describes a negative skill when one individual seeks to achieve at the expense of another.

Complacency is a trait that limits a person's actions because of fear or mental laziness.

Compression is a negative skill that narrows significantly a person's point of view or solution to an issue (see commitment).

Compromising is a skill set that seeks a win-win situation.

Conflict is an action of opposing ideas or positions.

Congruence is the skill to parallel through verbal and nonverbal communication another person's thinking and feeling.

Consideration is a skill that results in the perception of a focus on the group's needs.

Contingency is the rational preparation for change.

Cooperativeness is the degree an individual or a group will move from a position to the concerns of others.

Corporate values are a common set of beliefs held by the corporate stakeholders about their business environment.

Counseling is the skill to communicate on an interpersonal level so that the other person can resolve her or his own problems rather than through external advice or direction.

Creativity is the skill to take apparently unrelated data and to synthesize them into meaningful information.

Criticality is a position on the team where the individual in this situation has skills, usually technical, that if not available to the project, puts the project at risk.

A **cross-functional team** is the most common type of team for a corporate IT project, many technical and support groups with a multiple set of skills, ideas, goals, attitudes, and so forth.

Decoding is the communication process of interpreting data into information (see encoding).

Delegation is the skill to permit others to be responsible for tasks that you think you might be able to do better or are not functionally required to do.

Descriptive communication is the use of a descriptive (suggestive) technique rather than a prescriptive (do as you are told) technique to have a conversation.

Directive leadership is a skill set that uses as its guiding principle specific or prescriptive guidance.

Disciplining is a skill that is used in private to discourage negative deviation from the stated project goals.

Distortion is the misrepresentation of the situation whether it is a fact, experience, or a feeling.

Diversity is a mixture of personal cultures, gender, technical knowledge level, project experience, and group affiliation (IT, marketing, documentation, training, and so forth).

Effectiveness is the skill set required to define goals and to accomplish them.

Efficiency is the skill set that can accomplish with a minimum of input to get a maximum of output.

Empowerment is the skill to permit others to accomplish project tasks while at the same time achieving a balance between lack of power and abuse of power.

Encoding is the communication process of organizing data into information (see decoding).

Equity is a perception of project stakeholders that there is an equal sharing of workloads, rewards, and responsibilities.

Evaluation communication is a form of communication where values play the significant role of the judgment or of the importance of what is said by each actor, speaker or writer.

Expectation is a stated project goal that can become a perceived undocumented result.

Facilitator is the skill set required to oil the project's components to achieve effective and efficient results.

Feedback is an activity that should be held on a regular basis where the status of the person being evaluated can be clearly stated based on measurable standards or benchmarks.

Flexibility is the skill to exercise one's judgment rather than waiting for someone else to give direction.

Flexible communication is the conversation that permits the inclusion of additional data or alternatives to either resolve an issue or enhance a relationship.

Goal characteristics have to be measurable, specific, and potentially possible.

Goal selling is a strategy to influence others because of the value of the goal to the corporation and to themselves.

Goal setting is a skill set to establish measurable goals for project success and enhance, where applicable, project stakeholder performance.

A **group** is two or more individuals with corporate identity that is considered an entity.

Group dynamics is the rational and irrational interactions or behavioral patterns of a group (members to each other and the group to other groups).

Horizontal thinking is a type of thinking that stays within a management level or group to achieve a solution.

An **idea champion** is the manager type that permits an environment for creativity and innovation.

Ignoring is a negative skill that neglects both an employee's performance and emotional needs, that is, job satisfaction.

Imagination is a skill that can be observed when there are concrete results such as images, words, programming code, drawings, and so forth.

Imposing is the negative skill where there is only emphasis on the project stakeholder's performance (see indulging).

Indifference is a type of communication where one or both parties ignore the existence or importance of the other.

Indulging is the negative skill where there is only emphasis on the project stakeholder's satisfaction (see imposing).

Innovation is a significant change or breakthrough.

Integrating is the skill to merge project stakeholder performance and satisfaction equally (see imposing and indulging).

Integration is the technique of merging different groups into a coherent team to achieve a specific set of project goals.

Intergroup communication is communication between or among groups.

Interpersonal orientation is a position where the person uses a skill set based on people behavior and performance.

Interpersonal skill is a skill set that focuses on the human or people side of communicating or managing.

Intragroup communication is communication within a group.

An **interview** is a systematic and specialized process to determine if the candidate has the specific experiences and skills required to meet a measurable project goal.

Intuitive describes a skill that is observable in five forms from highest to lowest: person acts independently, person reports after the action, person recommends and then acts, the person asks for permission to act, and the person waits to be told.

Intuitive strategy is a method that uses an educated irrational position to establish direction or seek for relevancy among data elements.

Irrational problem solving is a set of skills that uses an intuitive (irrational) process for defining the problem or goal, generating alternative solutions, selecting the appropriate course, designing and developing the determined solution, validating the solution, and implementing the solution; not normally used in IT project management because of the need to use technical standards and benchmarks.

Leadership is a skill set that pulls people toward achievement rather than pushing them. It is a manager's ability to achieve.

Line-staff conflicts are differences of opinions and ideas between horizontal management levels.

Management is the process of working with people, resources, equipment, and materials to achieve organizational goals.

A **management review** is a regularly scheduled performance review.

Management team is a supervisory team that coordinates broad issues that affect the corporation.

Mediator uses the skill set required to intervene in a dispute between an "initiator" and a "responder."

Negotiator uses the skill set required in bargaining to achieve collaboration and accommodation to achieve a project goal.

Nonverbal communication is the skill set that uses body language to express what is desired, a form of message transmission that can be easily misinterpreted.

Open questions or imperative statements are the interview tactics to get general responses from the interviewee and do not include such imperatives as "Tell me about yourself."

Orchestrator is the skill set required to get project support, both internal and external, across cross-functional groups and all the various project stakeholder types.

An **organization** is an entity created to achieve what the separate individuals could not accomplish.

Organizational culture is a common set of assumptions, principles, processes, and structures held or used by members of a corporation, company, or even a project team.

Owned communication is the oral or written statements made that are considered the responsibility of the initiator (no aliases in e-mails).

Participative leadership is a type of leadership that uses team consultation before making a decision.

Perceptive describes the skill to use all five senses in making decisions.

Performance is the measurable level of action to achieve a measurable project goal.

A **performance interview** is feedback, a conversation based on the interviewee's performance (see performance).

Personality is a combination of a person's emotions, experiences, beliefs, and behavior.

A **probing response** is a type of question asked during an interview to clarify a candidate's earlier response.

Process is a systematic and sequential set of activities to achieve a set of measurable goals.

Process management is a set of skills required to plan, direct, assess, analyze, validate, and implement a systematic and sequential set of activities to achieve a set of measurable goals.

Project management is the process of working with people, resources, equipment, and materials to achieve project goals.

A **project team** is an organization put together to achieve a specific set of measurable goals with a specific time and with limited resources, equipment, and materials.

Projection is a negative skill to interpret the world totally based on one's own needs and desires.

Quality assurance is the component of quality control management that considers the deviations in performance during a project.

Quality control is the component of quality control management that considers the system or development processes of a project.

Quality control management is the process that seeks to prevent risks and if a risk occurs minimizes it.

Rational problem solving is a set of skills that uses an objective process for defining the problem or goal, generating alternative solutions, selecting the appropriate course, designing and developing the determined solution, validating the solution, and implementing the solution.

Rationalization is a negative skill to justify an apparent good reason rather than the real reason for an action.

Reassigning is putting a square peg that one tries first to fit into a round hole then more appropriately into a square hole; matching a skill level to where a positive performance can happen.

A **reflecting response** is an oral or a written confirmation of comprehension of the message that lead to acceptance or disapproval.

Retribution is a negative skill that uses a threat to influence, which usually results in a breakdown of relationships.

Rigid communication is a conversation in terms of absolutes that might be perceived as ultimatums.

A **risk** is a performance error that can have a significant or disastrous impact on the success of a project or major activity.

Risk analysis is a technique, tool, or method for assessing either quantitatively or qualitatively (or both) the impacts of an identified risk or a potential risk identified through a scenario.

Risk management is the management skill set where you identify a risk, assess a risk, and allocate resources to resolve the risk.

Role is a skill set with a label that perhaps explains the reasons for the actions and behavior of the actor.

Semantics is the core reason for conflict, word meanings, especially various meanings for the same word.

Specific goals are project goals that are measurable, unambiguous, and match exactly the customer's stated expectations.

The **sponsor** is the one who provides the resources and the working environment to make possible the achievement of project goals.

Stereotypes are assumptions about a group that usually have an irrational base.

Supportive communication is a conversation that is a sharing of information accurately so interpersonal relationships are not damaged.

A **system** is an interactive set of activities or groups that form a whole with dynamics that impact all the components.

Team is a group with a common purpose with skills that compliment each other.

Two-way communication is a conversation based on mutual respect, flexibility, and trust.

Verification communication is a conversation held to ensure comprehension of positions, a two-way conversation.

Vertical thinking is a type of thinking that crosses management levels to achieve a solution.

Index